COLLECTED WORKS OF
C. W. VALENTINE

Volume 3

T0418146

INTELLIGENCE TESTS
FOR CHILDREN

INTELLIGENCE TESTS
FOR CHILDREN

C. W. VALENTINE

Routledge
Taylor & Francis Group

LONDON AND NEW YORK

First published in 1945

This edition first published in 2015
by Routledge
27 Church Road, Hove BN3 2FA

and by Routledge
711 Third Avenue, New York, NY 10017

Routledge is an imprint of the Taylor & Francis Group, an informa business

British Library Cataloguing in Publication Data
A catalogue record for this book is available from the British Library

ISBN: 978-1-138-89931-5 (Set)
ISBN: 978-1-315-69276-0 (Set) (ebk)
ISBN: 978-1-138-89946-9 (Volume 3) (hbk)
ISBN: 978-1-315-70785-3 (Volume 3) (ebk)

Publisher's Note
The publisher has gone to great lengths to ensure the quality of this reprint but points out that some imperfections in the original copies may be apparent.

Disclaimer
The publisher has made every effort to trace copyright holders and would welcome correspondence from those they have been unable to trace.

INTELLIGENCE TESTS FOR CHILDREN

by

C. W. VALENTINE
M.A., D.Phil.

EMERITUS PROFESSOR IN THE
UNIVERSITY OF BIRMINGHAM

METHUEN & CO. LTD. LONDON
36 Essex Street, Strand, W.C.2

First published April 26th 1945
Second Edition January 1946
Third Edition, enlarged, May 1948
Fourth Edition, November 1949
Fifth Edition, revised, 1953

5.1

CATALOGUE NO. 3453/U

PRINTED AND BOUND IN GREAT BRITAIN
BY JARROLD AND SONS LTD. NORWICH

PREFACE TO FIFTH EDITION

It was suggested to me that the usefulness of this book would be increased if tests beyond those for 11-year-olds could be added, especially for use with pupils who are being considered for admission to Grammar Schools or Technical High Schools and for pupils in the Secondary Modern Schools. Accordingly in the third edition there were added tests for the ages of 12, 13, 14 and 15, which should provide ample material not only for the bright 11-year-olds but for all children up to 15. Among the new tests I included, as for earlier years, a number of Performance Tests. In the present edition further tests have been added for ages 14 and 15, and a few corrections and additions made elsewhere.

C. W. V.

The White House,
Wythall,
Nr. Birmingham.
Jan., 1953

NOTE

Apparatus for the tests in this book can easily be made in the school or home. But for Teachers who wish to test a considerable number of children, the publishers have provided specially made apparatus packed in an envelope which can be purchased separately, price 7s. 6d.; a list can be found on page 84. No instructions are provided in this envelope so that the apparatus can only be used in conjunction with this book. This special set of apparatus will not only save time, but will avoid the possible wearing or marking of diagrams, etc. in the book.

PREFACE TO FIRST EDITION

These tests are intended chiefly for teachers who wish to test children of about 2 to about 8 years of age, e.g. (*a*) children of Nursery School age (ages 2 to 5), (*b*) children at the Infant School (ages 5 to 7) or (*c*) children in the first year of the Junior School (ages 7 to 8), or (*d*) dull and backward children up to the age of 11.

It is highly desirable that every child should be tested as early as possible in his school life, that is, at the latest, on entering the Infant School or very soon after. The inborn intellectual deficiencies of the dull and even of some mental defectives may easily escape notice if the teacher trusts solely to the observation of ordinary behaviour. Sometimes, indeed, such children may give an impression of brightness by an engaging manner and anxiety to please. Others of stolid temperament may be regarded as lazy and punished accordingly, when in reality they are quite incapable of progressing at the same rate as their school-fellows: for example, I have recently had referred to me several juvenile delinquents who, I found, were on the border line of mental deficiency, and yet had passed through the ordinary elementary schools with reports that they were 'lazy'. Unfortunately testing often reveals children in the Junior and even Senior Schools who are on the border line of Mental Deficiency and should have had special treatment. The cases of backwardness are still more frequent and Burt has shown (in his book *The Backward Child*) that in over half such cases there is 'inborn general disability' though this factor is often overlooked. It is therefore particularly important that every backward child should be tested.

It is also important that as soon as possible the teacher should have some general idea as to how much can be expected of each child, so that, when practicable, the pupils can be divided into classes or at least groups of varying abilities, which can proceed at paces suited to their respective capacities.

No single testing can be regarded as final: the ideal is that a child should be tested while at the Nursery School or Kindergarten, again after entering the Infant School, and again shortly after he enters the Junior School. This will no doubt become an established custom in the near future, especially when the selection of pupils for various types of Secondary Schools comes to be based more on reports from the Junior Schools.

Of course, at these early ages, children must be tested individually and this takes time. But the teacher will be amply rewarded in the greater personal knowledge she gains, not only of the child's general intelligence and of some special abilities, but of his temperament.

For a precise assessment of a child's intelligence quotient —for the sake say of deciding whether he should be placed in a special school for mental defectives—the expert tester is needed, and usually more than one testing. But many teachers with some preliminary training in psychology can learn to apply tests of this kind with sufficient reliability to obtain a much better idea of the innate intelligence of their children than can be gained from general impressions, or even from the quality of the work in school, which may be so much affected by conscientiousness or indifference, by special home help and advantages or disadvantages.

Even an intelligent parent who knows nothing of intelligence tests should, if he obeys instructions strictly, and judges impartially, at least get a much better clue to the comparative intelligence of his own young children than he can by a vague comparison with those of a few friends.

The tests in this book require very little apparatus, and that can readily be found or made in the school or home. Many of the tests will be found entertaining by the children —who often beg to be tested again.

I wish to express my warm thanks to a number of authorities on the testing of children: to Professor Burt for allowing me to make full use of several of his own tests and of his extensive revisions of the Binet and Binet-Terman scales; to Professor Porteus for permission to include his Maze Tests;

to Dr. Arnold Gesell for giving me *carte blanche* in selecting any of his own tests; to Professor Terman and the publishers of the Terman-Merrill Tests for permission to use several of their tests; and to Dr. Alice Descoeudres and the authors of the Merrill-Palmer Tests for similar kindness.

I am also greatly indebted to several former research students and friends who have applied my tests in school and sent me detailed results. I owe special thanks to Mr. B. B. Wakelam, M.A., Headmaster of Moseley Road Infant and Junior School in Birmingham, who has personally tested over 250 children and supervised the testing of several of my students, and has also made a number of useful suggestions as to the wording of instructions, etc.; also to Mr. J. S. Flavell, M.A., Headmaster of Wheeler's Lane School, Birmingham, for similar generous help; to Mr. W. D. Wall, B.A., for applying the tests in a rural school and for some useful suggestions arising therefrom; to Miss M. Wright for testing a group in a Nursery School and checking results with her previous Terman-Merrill results; and to the following Heads for conducting or allowing testing in their schools in Birmingham; Miss D. A. Checketts, Selly Park Junior Mixed School; Miss E. M. Greenway, Bournville Infant School; Miss B. Castley, Deritend Nursery School; Miss M. Clarke, Greet Junior Mixed School; Miss A. S. Danby, the Edith Cadbury Nursery School.

Finally I want to thank again Professor Burt for reading the book in typescript with his usual generous expenditure of care and time, for his many helpful comments and particularly for helping me in the adaptation of a number of his own tests for a set of tests like the present.

C. W. V

Sept. 1944

CONTENTS

THE TESTS FOR VARIOUS AGES

 1. Either (a) Uses five or more words
    Or   (b) Spontaneously uses any two (recogniz-
    able) words in combination
 2. Has learnt to inhibit tendency to touch some for-
    bidden object without repeated command
 3. Bowel control
 4. Scribbles with crayon spontaneously or imitatively
 5. Unwraps a sweet
 6. Points to any one part of the body at a word
 7. Ball and box
 8. Imitates pronunciation of two words
 9. Uses a spoon
10. Walks alone

 1. Asks for some things (two at least) by recognizable
    names at table
 2. Bladder control
 3. Builds a tower
 4. Names three out of six common objects
 5. Formboard
 6. Uses appropriately two or three words in com-
    bination

INTRODUCTION

I. THE NATURE AND PURPOSE OF THE TESTS

Tests are here provided for children between the ages of $1\frac{1}{2}$ years and 15 years inclusive. As general, inborn intelligence increases very little, if at all, after 15 years, except in abler persons, these tests cover the whole range of intelligence in childhood.

In the building up of this new set of tests I have been guided by two main principles.

(1) Simplicity. No apparatus is needed except in a few tests, and for these it can easily be found or made with paper or cardboard in the school or home. Also the nature of procedure for each test can be readily grasped.

(2) Ample number and variety of tests. Thus, instead of the usual five or six Binet tests for each year, there are eight or ten tests for each year, up to age 8 inclusive. For the early years when development is taking place so rapidly, tests are provided for half-year intervals, i.e. $1\frac{1}{2}$, 2, $2\frac{1}{2}$, 3 and $3\frac{1}{2}$.

The fitting to the appropriate ages of the great majority of the well-known tests given here, has the support of at least two other investigators on Child Development, and especially (in addition to Binet for 3 years and onwards), Professor Sir Cyril Burt, Dr. Arnold Gesell, and the recent Terman and Merrill scales. In addition the tests have been applied as a set to about 580 children chiefly of the ages of 4 ; o to 7 ; o or 8 ; o. (See Appendix.)

For the earliest years (i.e. $1\frac{1}{2}$ to 3 years) I have especially chosen those tests which I have found best in testing, over a period of some fifteen years, my own children, and those of friends, from the age of twelve months onwards.

When two reliable investigators differ somewhat in the placing of a test, or in the score required, I have sometimes made a compromise unless a good reason appeared for choosing one rather than the other; but I have always adopted Burt's revision of the Binet-Terman placings where available, except for one or two tests specially referred to in the Appendix.

These tests are primarily meant to afford a preliminary estimate of the general stage of development. Though the testing of *general intelligence* is the main purpose, various aspects of development are involved. The tests involve *special abilities* as well as general intelligence. Consequently a child's failure in one type of test prescribed for his age must not be taken as indicating lack of general intelligence. Thus a child who is comparatively slow in developing language in the pre-school years, may reveal good intelligence in doing tests in which language is not important; and he may prove to be above average general intelligence later on. One of my own children, for example, was rather slow in linguistic development at 2 and 3 years of age; and yet he afterwards was declared on being tested by the National Institute of Industrial Psychology to be well up to the average of University students in general intelligence.

As, however, either eight or ten tests are provided for each of the years or half-years $1\frac{1}{2}$ to 8 and six tests for ages 9 to 13, and as each child will probably attempt the tests prescribed for three, four or five successive years (or half-years), a great variety of tests will be given to each child. Hence the result will depend *chiefly* on his 'general intelligence' because that is involved in each test.[1] So far as we are testing special abilities (e.g. verbal ability or facility in dealing with numbers, or any specific ability involved in reasoning) we are testing abilities which will be important later on.

Elements of *character and temperament* and the degree of social development also enter in. It is impossible to eliminate these entirely from any tests, especially at these early ages. Thus willingness to co-operate, obedience, suggestibility,

---

[1] That in the early years general ability is a far more important factor than special abilities in intelligence tests and in school work, is stressed by Burt (see his *Mental and Scholastic Tests*, and his article, 'The Education of the Adolescent', *Brit. Jour. of Educ. Psych.*, Vol. XIII). On special abilities in early childhood see C. W. Valentine, *Psychology and its bearing on Education*. Chap. XXIV (Methuen, 1950).

calmness and self-control instead of fluster and hurry, persistence instead of immediate abandonment of effort in face of a difficulty—all these may affect the performance. Indeed one of the advantages of individual tests of this kind is that they may reveal a good deal about the character and temperament of the child to a stranger, and sometimes even to a parent. It was surprising to me, for example, to note how one of my children—with a quick, alert mind, was pulled up in some of the earlier Maze Tests by being so impulsive, while another child who was slower in many of the tests, scored an advantage through his greater caution.[1]

Shyness, nervousness and unwillingness to co-operate affect especially the performance of many children under 4 ; o, or 5 ; o, and that is no doubt the chief reason why estimates of intelligence below 4 or 5 years of age are so much less reliable than they are a few years later.

Even the tester with some experience in intelligence testing should have some practice with these particular tests before he relies confidently on the results he obtains, and he should begin his practice with children he knows to be fairly average, leaving till later when he is thoroughly familiar with the tests, the dull and backward or 'difficult children' and especially any suspected of being on the border line of mental deficiency.

II. THE DETECTION OF DULL OR MENTALLY DEFICIENT CHILDREN

This set of tests may be taken as suitable for placing the teacher's own pupils in a fairly reliable order of merit in intelligence, to select those of superior or of dull intelligence, and to give a preliminary selection of possible mental deficients. But no single testing, even by an expert, should definitely label a young child 'mentally defective', nor should the intelligence-quotient based on this set of tests

[1] On the value of the Maze Tests see p. 69 ; also *The Maze Test and Mental Differences*, by S. D. Porteus (Vineland, New Jersey, 1933), and *Mental and Scholastic Tests*, by Cyril Burt, 2nd edition, 1947, p. 254.

2

be taken as precisely equivalent to that based on others. If on the basis of these tests a child appears to be near the border line of mental deficiency (say with an Intelligence Quotient below about 75) he should be retested by an expert with a more widely standardized set of tests, e.g. Burt's revision of the Binet-Terman Tests, or the Terman-Merrill Tests when revised for British children.

In the Appendix will be found a fuller discussion, intended for the psychologist, of the tests selected and of their placing, of the new tests introduced and their standardization, and of the preliminary results of the applications of this set of tests.

III. PROCEDURE AND IMPORTANT POINTS IN TESTING

(1) The child must be in good physical condition—not tired, sleepy or hungry. A serious illness may affect performance for some time after.

(2) Test each child for a short time only, varying according to age: e.g. twenty minutes is usually enough for a five-year-old. If the child appears bored, change the test or have an interval of play, or defer until another time. It is important that the tester should maintain an attitude of keen interest himself. To the child the tests should be referred to as 'puzzles' or games. It is a help if the various pieces of apparatus are kept in several gaily coloured boxes and the child allowed to open them in turn.

(3) Ideally the tester should be known and liked by the child. The first children tested should be the most confident, talkative type; their reactions will reassure any nervous ones.

(4) The tester should have the child in a separate room; but if he is a stranger to the child it will probably be helpful, and even necessary when the child is very young—say only two or three—to have the mother or a known and liked teacher present. But they must be told emphatically not to try to help the child.

If no separate room is available, take the child at the back of the room with his back to the class.

(5) The tester should first get on good terms by playing with the child, or in the case of very little ones, by leaving them to play with some toy while paying them very little attention.

(6) In order to get quickly a rough idea of the intelligence of the child, begin with the *starred tests* only. These are usually tests which take little time and are specially well standardized.

(7) Begin with the starred tests prescribed for the age period just *below* that of the child tested, to give him confidence. Thus with a three-year-old begin with starred tests for 2½ years. If he fails in one of these go back to the 2-year tests. Continue with later tests until he fails in one of the starred tests for any given age. If a child is nervous or very diffident it is well to give two or three very easy tests to start with, prescribed for children two or three years younger.

(8) Having found roughly by the starred tests, the mental level of the child, proceed to give all the other tests for the age *below* that at which the child failed one of the starred tests. If he fails one of these go back to the tests for the age below that, until you find the age at which he passes *all* the tests prescribed for that age.

(9) Now give all the tests above this age (not already attempted) until you reach an age group at which the child only does *one* of the tests for that year.

(10) Give an encouraging smile or say 'good' to a child as he finishes each test—whether right or wrong. An exception to this must be made in tests where there are several items to be given, e.g. in 'Definitions' and 'Description of pictures'. If the first answer is of the wrong type, to praise it would encourage a continuance of answers of that type. Rather say: 'Well, not quite right; see if you can do better with the next.' So with repetition of numbers and words: if the first answer is wrong say: 'Well, not quite right—try this one.'

(11) Be extremely careful *not* to give any sign to the child at any point in the middle of a test when he seems to be hesitating, especially in such tests as the Formboard, all the Maze Tests, No. 1 and No. 8 for 4 ; o, No. 6 for 5 ; o, No. 9 for age 6 ; o. A child will often watch your face for a sign whether he is doing the test correctly.

(12) Do not correct the child or give him the right answer except where instructed to do so; for he may inform other children who are to be tested later. Also it is desirable to retest the child after an interval and the same tests may be needed. At the earliest ages (1 and 2 years) the tests may be repeated after a week or two. At 3 and 4 the intervals should be a month or two, with increasing intervals thereafter. Estimates of intelligence are more reliable if based upon several testings, especially if these are spread over a period of one or more years.[1]

(13) Distrust a very low result, because the child may be distracted, tired, or in a playful mood, etc. Therefore retest after a few weeks, assuming you have not told the child the correct answers. High results can be trusted more fully (unless you have gone beyond instructions or used suggestions), except when the child has been exceptionally lucky in those tests in which there is an element of chance.

(14) It is essential that the tester should adhere strictly to the instructions as to procedure and scoring. Do not say to yourself, 'Oh, the child really could do that if he understood what to do'. The child's ability to *under-*

---

[1] When the same tests are applied after only a short interval some improvement in performance is expected merely as the result of practice. Thus one investigator with group tests found that the Mean Intelligence Quotient of a large group of children increased from 106 at the first testing to 113 at the second, made a week later with a similar set of tests; but there was very little change in four further testings. See D. M. McIntosh, *Brit. Jour. of Educ. Psych.*, Vol. XIV, 1944, and in Vols. XXI and XXII, articles by E. A. Peel. Terman and Merrill found that the giving of their parallel test M only a few days after giving test L (or vice versa) resulted in an increase of only 3 I.Q. points for ages 2 to 4 ; 6, and 2 points for ages 5 to 16. (*Measuring Intelligence*, p. 43.) These tests are individual tests similar to those in this book.

stand the instructions is often an important part of the test. So do not give supplementary *hints* to the child beyond those given in the instructions.

Instructions may have to be repeated, however, if the child is slightly deaf. Preliminary conversation should give a warning of this. Always speak slowly so that the child can easily follow. Beware also of the child being unable to understand because of his dialect.

(15) Before beginning testing, prepare a record sheet for the child with the numbers of the tests in order so that you can at once insert the score for each test as you proceed. Until you are thoroughly familiar with the tests, write down the child's replies as he goes along if there is the slightest doubt as to their correctness, leaving consideration of the scoring till later. Where the scoring of a test leaves much to the judgment of the tester it would be helpful to read the fuller suggestions as to satisfactory and unsatisfactory answers given in Burt's *Mental and Scholastic Tests* or Terman and Merrill's *Measuring Intelligence*, if the test is included in one of those books. References will be given to selected tests later for this purpose.

(16) In a few tests, especially such as that on Differences (age 6 ; 0, No. 5) and that on Definitions, there is a danger that a child will report to others what he has been asked and what he said. So far as possible arrange that a child will not be able to communicate with others who are to be tested that same morning or afternoon. There is some compensation in the fact that it is only the more intelligent child who is likely to concern himself with what is being asked and to take note of answers.

(17) '*Problem Children.*' If a child remains persistently uncooperative even when the tester is no longer a stranger, it is possible that emotional causes are a special hindrance. These may be partly innate and partly environmental. An improvement in environment (e.g. removal from a bad home) sometimes results in a marked increase

in the Intelligence Quotient in the course of time. The revelation of emotional inhibitions is one of the values of individual testing. If these can be got rid of in the testing, a level of intelligence may be revealed in a backward child which shows that his school work must be suffering from emotional hindrances.

(18) The Performance Tests, involving little or no use of language by the child (including a few in which the child does not actually perform an action) are marked with a P so that the score on these can be readily compared with the score on the more verbal tests.

(19) Of course any *apparatus* needed should be prepared beforehand. It is listed at the end of each year-group of tests.

IV. MENTAL AGE AND INTELLIGENCE QUOTIENT

Success in each test scores 1. If a child of 6 years does all the tests for his age, then he is at least up to the average of children of that age. Any successes in tests beyond that age (say, for ages 7 and 8) would then put him ahead of the average child of 6. For example, if he does all the seven-year-old tests and none beyond, his mental level is about that of the average seven-year-old, and his *Mental Age* is said to be 7.

If after doing all the 6-year tests, he does six of the 7-year tests but misses two, he makes up for those two misses if he does two of the 8-year tests; that would again make his mental age at least 7. If he does any further tests that puts his mental age still higher.

As explained in the section on Procedure, if the six-year-old misses some of the 6-year tests then still earlier tests should be tried, till you find a stage at which he passes *all*. Then the calculation of mental age can start from this as a basis. If he does all the 5-year tests we can start from the basic age of 5. For example, suppose he scores as follows:

    5-year tests. All passed. Basic mental age 5.
    6-year tests. 7 out of 10 passed.
    7-year tests. 4 out of 8 passed.
    8-year tests. 1 out of 6 passed.

The 4 tests passed at 7 ; 0 make up for the 3 misses at 6 ; 0 and leave 1 over. With the one passed at 8 ; 0 this gives him 2 beyond the 6 year level. This is regarded as equivalent to 2 out of the 8 tests for 7 ; 0. As $\frac{2}{8} = \frac{1}{4}$ the boy's mental age is $6\frac{1}{4}$. (Note that for this purpose no greater credit is given for passing an 8-year test than for a 7-year test.)

The calculation is similar when half-years are concerned. Thus if a child does all the 3-year tests, four of the eight tests for 3 ; 6 and one of those for 4 ; 0, this counts as five of the tests towards the 8 for 3 ; 6; i.e. as $\frac{5}{8}$ of *half* a year, i.e. $\frac{5}{16}$ of a year. So his mental age is $3\frac{5}{16}$ or just over $3\frac{1}{4}$ years.

Intelligence Quotient. Having obtained the mental age of the child it is now only a matter of arithmetic to get his intelligence quotient, which is his *mental* age divided by his *real* age. Thus suppose the age of the six-year-old we have been considering was precisely 6 ; 0, then we proceed as follows:

Boy's real age—6 years. Boy's mental age—$6\frac{1}{4}$ years.

$$\text{Intelligence quotient} = \frac{\text{mental age}}{\text{real age}} = \frac{6\frac{1}{4}}{6} = \frac{25}{24} = 1\cdot04.$$

The I.Q. is usually expressed as a percentage, so it becomes 104, i.e. just above the average, which is 100. If the boy's real age were 6 years and 5 months his I.Q. would be

$$\frac{6\frac{1}{4}}{6\frac{5}{12}} = \frac{25}{4} \times \frac{12}{77} = \frac{75}{77} = 0\cdot97,$$ or expressed as a percentage, 97,

i.e. just below the average.

The majority of children have an I.Q. of between about 85 and 115 on well standardized scales; an I.Q. around 65–70 or less would indicate that the child is probably suited for a Special School for defectives. We know, however, that the I.Q. varies somewhat with the type of tests used, and the level of tests given in this book must not at present be taken as precisely equivalent to that of Burt's revision of the Binet scale or of the newer Terman and

---

[1] A useful diagram showing distribution of I.Q.'s based on the Terman and Merrill tests is given in their book, *Measuring Intelligence*, p. 41.

Merrill tests, though the number of tests in common is substantial, and the difficulty of the other tests I have included for the various ages corresponds closely to that of the tests which are also in the Binet or Terman scales.

V. VALIDITY OF TESTS FOR THE FIRST TWO OR THREE YEARS

It is not yet certain how far tests for the first two or three years or so are dependable as prophecies of later years, except very roughly. Mental deficiency can often be detected by the end of the first year and sometimes even in the first few months.[1] We also know that many men of genius have shown signs of precocity by the end of the first year or two.[2] On the other hand, in some cases (not very numerous when the tests have been accurately done) considerable changes have taken place in the estimates of the general intelligence of the same child at various ages: thus some highly gifted children (who later had an Intelligence Quotient of over 150) have shown no precocity in walking or talking.[3] I have found very close correspondence in my own five children between very early tests (at only 12 or even 6 months) with tests of their intelligence at 10 years and later. It has been very striking to find so similar an Intelligence Quotient for the same child by such tests as are given here for 1½, 2, and 3 years and later by Binet and other tests at 5, 10 and 12 years of age.

A few children are of course of no value for generalization and this constant testing (especially the observation of first appearances and the gradual and even intermittent nature of development), has brought home to me strongly how much depends upon the particular conditions at the time of testing, especially with the very young. When these are not kept constant it is not surprising if different results are gained

[1] Gesell gives some remarkable examples of mental deficiency detected in the first six months: see his *Infancy and Human Growth*.

[2] See C. M. Cox, *Genetic Studies of Genius*, Vol. II (edited by L. M. Terman), 1926.

[3] See L. Hollingworth, *Gifted Children* (New York), 1929.

at different times with the same set of tests.[1] In addition, the great influence of emotional mood and of the child's relation to the tester make it essential that several testings, preferably at intervals of several months shall be made before a final estimate of the child's intelligence is made.

Summing up we may say that inferences as to probable later intelligence must be made with special caution if based only on tests at 2 ; 0 and 2 ; 6 or thereabouts, and never on the basis of only one testing. Nevertheless we can at least say, on the basis of performances in these tests, that certain things are done by, say, 50 or 60 per cent of children at 2 years and by 90 per cent at 3 years.

Parents must not be worried by deficiency in one or two particular tests, nor do we as yet know enough to say that slowness in most acquirements may not be compensated to some extent by more rapid development later, though this certainly seems to be very rare. Furthermore, in the first year or two it is possible that environment, correct feeding, and sympathetic companionship may have a more stimulating effect than they have later; and varying conditions at the time of testing may affect results even more.[2]

A further note on the validity of tests at 2 ; 0 and 3 ; 0 is given in the Appendix, p. 78.

When we come to the ages of 4 ; 0 and 5 ; 0 we find tests much more dependable and more closely predictive of general intelligence at 10 ; 0 or 12 ; 0. Indeed one headmaster (Mr. B. B. Wakelam) who tested 250 young children with these tests found a correlation of 0·81 between test results and *educational attainment* at 8 ; 0 [3].

[1] I have discussed conflicting evidence as to the prophetic reliability of Gesell's Tests for one- or two-year-olds in my book, *The Psychology of Early Childhood: a Study of Mental Development in the First Years of Life* (Methuen, 1942), Chapter I. There I have also given further particulars of the results gained with my own children. I have also given evidence of the *intermittence* of mental development in infancy—which results in a child rising to a certain level of development in, say, reasoning, once or twice in a certain day, and then not reaching it again for some weeks, and so on with decreasing intervals.

[2] See F. L. Goodenough, *The Kuhlmann-Binet Tests for Children of Pre-School Age* (Minneapolis, 1928).

[3] See footnote, p. 74.

THE TESTS FOR VARIOUS AGES

TESTS FOR AGE 1 ; 6

1. *Either* (a) *Uses five or more words*, additional to Mama and Dadda; e.g. ta, baby, bow-bow, gone. (Some days of careful observation may be needed to note these. Anything recognizably meant for the word should score, e.g. baba, go(ne).)
   Or (b) *Spontaneously uses any two (recognizable) words in combination*, e.g. Daddy gone; drink milk; open door. Test 1 scores 1 if either (a) *or* (b) is passed.

2. *Has learnt to inhibit tendency to touch some forbidden object without repeated command.*

3. *Bowel control* (with only occasional lapses).

4. *Scribbles with crayon spontaneously or imitatively.* Give the child a crayon and paper. If he does not scribble, you do so and give him the crayon again with an appropriate gesture.

5. *Unwraps a sweet.* Show a red, yellow or pink sweet to the child and touch his lips and tongue with it. Now wrap the sweet up in soft paper, so that it remains covered, but not doubly wrapped. Give it to the child. Passed if child gets at the sweet.

6. *Points to any one point of the body at a word.* Say: 'Show me your mouth', 'hand', 'toes', etc.

7. *Ball and Box.* Provide a box about one foot square (or a round waste-paper basket about one foot across) and a ball or brick small enough for child to grasp. Throw the ball in the box: take it out and give it to the child saying: 'You put the ball in the box.'
   Passed if thrown in by the child while sitting, or dropped in while standing. Allow *three* trials.

8. *Imitates* the pronunciation of two out of ten words which he has often heard but has not yet learned to say

spontaneously. (Any recognizable imitation should pass.)

9. *Uses a spoon* without much spilling, getting some food into the mouth.

10. *Walks alone* more than three steps without any help.

TESTS FOR AGE 2 ; 0

1. *Asks for some things (two at least) by recognizable names at table.*

2. *Bladder control.* Normal—occasional lapses allowed.

*3.[1] *Builds a tower.* Tester builds a tower of four or five bricks and says: 'You make one like this.' The child must build a tower of at least four bricks, so that it will **(P)** stand for a moment. The blocks should be about an inch square, easy to take hold of and yet not too hard to stand one on another.

4. *Names three out of six common objects.* Select only objects the child has often heard named and handled, for example spoon, cup, door, pussy, chair. Point to each in turn and ask: 'What's that?'

5. *Formboard.* Take a sheet of thick cardboard about 6 inches by 9. Cut out a circle, a square and a triangle— **(P)** each about 1½ inches across, arranged as below. Trim these shapes so that each will fit easily into its hole.

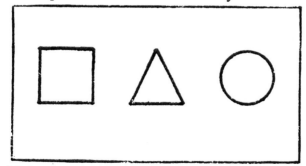

Make the child watch you as you put the blocks in the right holes. Remove the blocks and place each on the

---

[1] For explanation of stars here and in later tests see Introduction, p. 5.

table *before its proper hole.* Now say: 'Now you put them all back in their own holes.'

All must be placed correctly but the block need not be fitted right in: it is enough if it is placed over the hole in the right position. If the child shows that he is satisfied and yet has not placed all three blocks correctly, place them all on the table again and demonstrate a second time. Give a second trial but no more.

Passed if all the blocks are placed correctly even if only on the second trial.

*6. *Uses appropriately two or three words in combination* to make a simple sentence. (Any two words put together will do—e.g. 'Mummy hat', 'Daddy gone'.)

7. *Folds paper once.* A piece of paper (about note-paper size) is folded once or twice while the child is watching. A similar piece is now given to the child, who is told:

(P)   'You do it.'

One fold scores success. Repeat *once* if necessary.

8. *Prepositions understood.* Understands and carries out two orders (involving prepositions) out of these five: 'Put the pencil *on* the box', '*in* the box', '*behind*', '*in front of*', '*under*'.

*9. *Obeys simple commands.* Put before the child three or four objects very familiar to him. Give three simple commands, one at a time; e.g. say (1) 'Give me the

(P)   spoon'; (2) 'Put the ball in the cup'; (3) 'See this box? Put it on the chair.' The request may be repeated several times. *Two* must be done out of three.

10. *Imitates any interesting action,* for example, reading, smoking, a funny walk, or, in response to mother or well-known teacher or nurse, 'waves handy', or claps her hands, or nods her head.

The test is passed if *one* action is clearly imitated.

Apparatus needed: Building blocks, six common objects, formboard, piece of paper, crayon and paper, sweet and paper, ball or cube, small box.

TESTS FOR AGE 2 ; 6

*1. *Formboard.* Use the same board as for age 2 ; o, test 5. If that test has not already been done it should be given now as prescribed for age 2 ; o. If the child fails to do **(P)** that test then he reckons as failing in this test for 2 ; 6. If he fits the figures correctly take them out and place each on the table opposite its appropriate hole. Now turn the board half-way round on the table (so that the apex of the hole for the triangle is now towards the child) while the child watches. Now say: 'Put them back again in the right holes.'

If he fails, repeat the procedure and give him a second trial. The discs should be fitted right into their holes at this age.

*2. *Pointing to parts of the body.* Say (1) 'Show me your nose'; (2) 'Show me your eyes'; (3) 'Show me your hair'; (4) 'Show me your mouth'; (5) 'Show me your knee'. *Three* out of five to be pointed to correctly.

3. *Naming four out of six common objects.* Select only objects which the child has often handled, or at least seen and heard named, e.g. spoon, cup, chair, fire, pussy, door, bed. Point to the object and say: 'What is that?'

4. *Fetching scissors and cutting paper.* Tell the child to watch you while you take a pair of scissors and make a cut in a **(P)** sheet of paper of large note-paper size. Put the scissors some way off and say: 'Now fetch the scissors and cut the paper. Do what I did.'   Help the child to take hold of the scissors if necessary.

The test is passed if the child makes any cut in the paper.

*5. *Identifying objects by use.* Put five objects on a tray: a cup, shoe, penny, knife, hairbrush, and nearby stand a chair. Say: 'Show me what we drink out of.' The child must point to the cup. Then, 'Show me what goes on your feet', 'what we can buy things with', 'what cuts bread', 'what you can do your hair with', 'what we sit on'. The test is passed if *three* are indicated. Naming correctly does not score by itself; pointing is essential.

6. *Tells experiences.* Get the child to talk, and, by questioning, see if he can relate some simple experience.
The test is passed if this is done, even in broken sentences.

7. *Repeats three syllables.* Say: 'Listen; say this after me: "Mama".' When the child has responded, continue with (1)' Dear Mama', and so if necessary with (2) 'Good pussy', and (3) 'Come in, Daddy'. Do not say anything that is not true (e.g. 'It's raining') or that the child would naturally not want to say, e.g. 'Smack me'.)
Any one pair of words repeated (containing three syllables in the pair) scores a pass.

8. *Use* (a) *of the pronoun 'I' or 'you':* (b) *of a past tense, and* (c) *of a plural form.* If the tester is a stranger and he cannot get absolutely reliable reports, he must lead the conversation so that such forms would be used if known. The test is passed if two out of the three (a), (b), and (c) are used.
Apparatus needed: Formboard, six common objects, scissors and paper.

TESTS FOR AGE 3 ; 0

*1. *Formboard.* As for 2 ; 6, No. 1, but now repeat the test with the rotated formboard even if the blocks are placed
(P)   correctly the first time.
Both trials must now be passed to score 1.

*2. *Names parts of the face and body.* Say: 'Show me (1) your nose'; (2) 'your eyes'; (3) 'your mouth'; (4) 'your hair'; and (5) 'your knee'. Repeat the request as often as necessary.
Four parts to be named out of five.

3. *Puts on own shoes.* As this is so dependent upon training the children should, if necessary, be given a short
(P)   demonstration and trial before the final test. One shoe should be put on completely, but the laces need not be tied.

4. *Copies a circle.* Show a circle already drawn and ask the
(P)   child to make one like it. Place the model on the table in
front of him but do not let him see you draw it.
The test is passed if more than half the circle is completed in a curve. *Three* attempts allowed.

5. *Prepositions understood.* As in 2 ; 0, No. 8, but *three* out
of five are required now.

6. *Action Agent.* Ask: 'What runs?' If a correct answer
is given, say: 'Good, what cries?' If a correct answer is
given, give the following similarly. If a good answer
is not given to 'What runs?' say: 'A boy runs, doesn't he?'
If no answer is given to 'What cries?' then proceed with
'What sleeps?' and others in the following list with no
more hints.

1. sleeps	6. burns	11. sails	16. gallops
2. scratches	7. cuts	12. boils	17. aches
3. flies	8. blows	13. floats	18. explodes
4. bites	9. shoots	14. growls	19. roars
5. swims	10. melts	15. stings	20. mews

Eight to be answered correctly of the numbered list to
score 1. Four words right score a half.

7. *Garden path.* Say, 'This is a garden path' (running your
dry pen round from S back again). 'You must not go on
(P)   the grass; so you must not touch the lines. You come
into the garden here (pointing to S) and go right round
(tracing slowly with pen) and come out here again.'
Demonstrate this twice, bringing the pen right out at S.
The child must use a dry pen. (See next page for diagram.)
The test is passed if the child does not cross a line or
cut off a corner in more than three places in any one trial.
Three trials are allowed. Success on one of these trials
scores 1. Success on a fourth trial scores a half.

N.B. The child must turn his pen out of the exit at
the end or it counts as one error towards three. He may
be allowed to go round two or even three times before
coming out, but each crossing of the line counts as an
error.

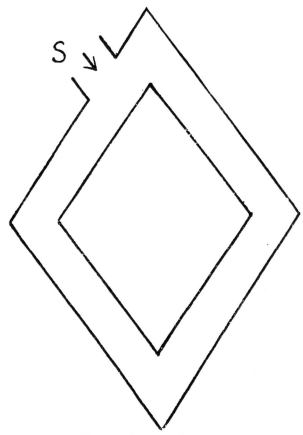

*8. *Repeating numbers.* 'I am going to say some numbers. Listen and say them after me—3, 7, 4.' Pronounce each number very distinctly at the rate of one per second. If the response is wrong give three other numbers.

The test is passed if one is right out of four trials.

Apparatus needed: Formboard, shoes, pencil and paper, pen.

TESTS FOR AGE 3 ; 6

*1. *Pictures—names two objects in each.* Select two further pictures similar to the one provided here (i.e. a street

3

scene, with shops, motor cars, etc., a house scene with children playing, a country scene, a shop scene, or a playground scene.) The pictures must be understandable to the child. Say to the child: 'Tell me about this picture.' Do the same with the other two pictures. Two objects must be named in each picture. If this is only done for two pictures score ½. The mere naming of objects scores.

*2. *Putting together two cut halves of a picture.* Material: two cards, about picture-postcard size, each with a picture of a well-known animal (dog, cat, or horse) cut vertically **(P)** about the middle of the animal. The size of the animal in the picture should not be less than about 2 inches. Of course the two pictures should be of two different animals.

Place the two halves of the picture thus:

Say: 'Put these together to make a dog.'
The test is passed if *one* is done correctly. The outlines of the animals need not be placed by the child exactly in line, but if they are not the cards must touch. If the cards do not touch the figures must be in line.

3. *Repeats six syllables.* Ask: 'Can you say "Daddy"?' After the reply continue: 'Listen and say this after me, "My hat and shoes".' (This is for practice.) Now get these repeated after you:

    (*a*) I'd like to have a cake.
    (*b*) Please give me a pencil.
    (*c*) Some big pussies catch mice.
One in three (*a*, *b*, or *c*) must be exactly correct.

4. *Colour sorting*. Put three small saucers on the table in front of the child. Place in the first a patch of white **(P)** paper, in the second a patch of black paper, and in the third a patch of red paper. Provide also three similar patches of each of the three colours. (Counters or beads or buttons may be used instead.) Taking a black, say: 'See, this one goes in this saucer with the one like it.' Then take the white, 'And this goes here with the one like it.' (So with the red.) 'Now you put all these other colours (mixing them) in their right saucers with the others like them.'

Allow a child to take a paper out if he realizes his own mistake. A full mark is scored if the child sorts all correctly; $\frac{1}{2}$ if there is only one error.

5. *Folds a paper twice*. Take a piece of letter-sized paper. Tell the child to watch you. Fold the paper and then **(P)** fold it again at right-angles. Hand a new piece to the child and say: 'Now you do that.'

Both folds are needed to score, but the edges need not be exactly in line.

6. *Either* (a) *goes on simple errands outside the house*. This test will no doubt favour children from poorer homes. **(P)** But most of the language tests favour those from better homes. An alternative is provided for use in schools when the tester has not reliable information about the child.

Or (b) *social and dramatic play*. The child is able to take part in acting-play, something more than mere imitation of a single action such as required in test 10 for 2 ; o. For example, he co-operates in playing at shop and acts as buyer or salesman, or acts the doctor or mother when baby (or doll) is ill. (This test is rather easy as compared with (a). If used it must be strictly interpreted.)

7. *Understands 'Two'*. Put several buttons or matches on the table with a cup. Say: 'Put *one* button in the cup (stressing "one").' If this is done right take it out and say, 'Good! Now put *two* buttons in the cup.' If this is

done correctly repeat both orders to make sure the difference between 'one' and 'two' is understood.
No error is allowed.

8. *Matching geometric figures.*

(P) The tester should trace the figures on p. 23 on ten separate, small, square pieces of paper. Select the vertical line, point to the figures opposite and say: 'You see all these things?' Then put your separate vertical line on the small cross (X) and say: 'Now you see this one' (pointing). Find me another just the same as this.' Correct a first error, saying: 'No: find one just the same as this.'

Make no comment on further errors, but pass on to the next figure. Take the triangle second, the circle third, and the rest haphazard.

Five out of ten figures must be matched correctly to pass.

Apparatus needed: Pictures, two picture postcards of animals, three small saucers, white, black and red paper (or similar coloured counters or buttons), paper, geometric figures on paper.

TESTS FOR AGE 4 ; 0

*1. *Comparing two lines.* Say: 'You see these two lines. Show me which is the longer.' After the child has pointed to one, remove this page from his sight, turn it upside down and repeat the test. Then turn it back again and repeat
(P) again.

The correct answer must be given each time to score.

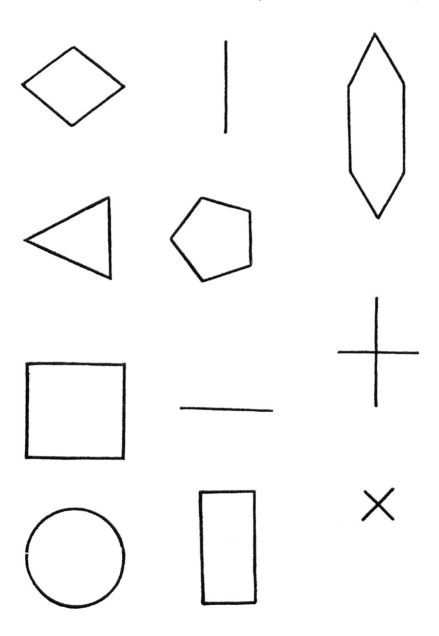

*2. *Counting.* Put four pennies on the table, arranged roughly as a square. Say: 'You see these pennies? Count them and tell me how many there are.' If necessary say, 'Count them with your finger like this'—pointing and counting 1—2 . . .
Two trials can be allowed.

3. *Repeating eight syllables.* Ask: 'Can you say "Mummy"?' After the reply say: 'Listen and say this after me: "My coat and stockings".' (This is for practice.) Now get the child to repeat the following:
    (*a*) It is often cold and rainy.
    (*b*) I like to eat cake and biscuits.
    (*c*) A pussy cat loves to catch mice.
Two out of three (*a*, *b*, or *c*) must be *perfectly* correct.

4. *Matching geometric designs.* As for 3 ; 6, No. 8, but eight
(P) out of ten figures must now be matched correctly. If eight were done when doing the tests for 3 ; 6 that scores a pass here again.

5. *Comprehends questions.* Say:
    (*a*) 'Why do we have houses?' (Anything which shows understanding of some use passes, e.g. 'To live in', 'For people', 'To play', 'To sleep in'.)
    (*b*) 'What should you do when you are cold?' (Allow 'Go to bed', as in poor homes, or with a coal shortage it may be the best thing to do!)
    (*c*) What should you do when you are hungry?
Two sensible answers out of three are required.

6. *Maze.* Give the Garden Path test for 3 ; 0 first unless already given.
(P) Proceed with this 4 ; 0 test in the same way. A dry pen must be used. Two trials are allowed; in each case the child's pen may not go round more than twice without coming out at S.
The test is passed in either of the two trials if the child does not cross the line more than twice in the one trial.

7. *Action Agent.* As for 3 ; 0, No. 6, but thirteen answers are now required out of twenty.

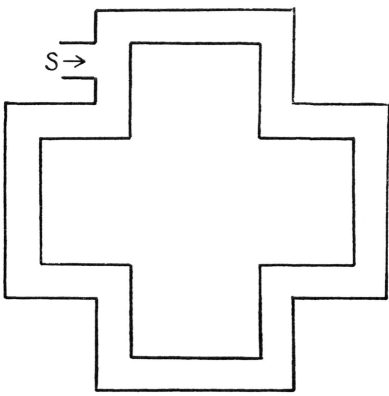

8. *Comparing faces.* (See next page.) Show the child the first pair of faces, covering the rest. Say: 'Tell me which of these is the prettier?' (Do not point to either yourself.) Repeat the question once (if necessary) for each pair.

All three must be chosen correctly at the first attempt.

Apparatus needed: Four pennies, geometric figures on paper, pen.

TESTS FOR AGE 5 ; 0

1. Morning or afternoon. Ask: 'Is it morning or afternoon now?' (The midday meal may be taken as the dividing line.) If answered correctly this question should be repeated at the end of the tests for this year. The answers must be right *both* times to score.

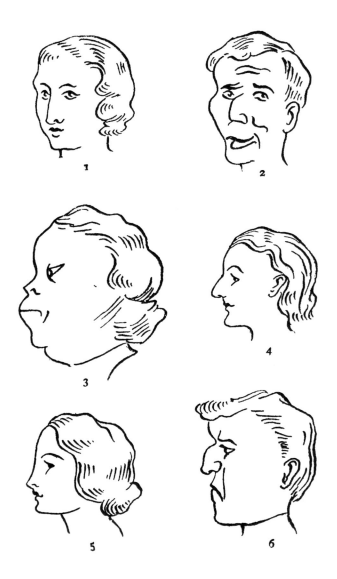

*2. *Drawing of a man.* The child is asked to draw a man. It should be clearly recognizable, but straight lines may serve for limbs. If the child stops after drawing the head, (P) say: 'I want the whole man drawn.'

Scoring: Start with 1 if at all recognizable.

Take off ¼ mark for any limb not represented.

Take off ¼ mark for any part disconnected or far from the appropriate place.

Take off ¼ mark if signs for at least three of these are not given: (a) both eyes (or one if the drawing is in profile), (b) mouth, (c) nose, (d) both ears (or one if in profile).

Take off ¼ mark if the body is not completed. Against these add ¼ mark for any sign of clothing and ¼ mark for hair, but the maximum mark is 1.

*3. *Repeating* 12 *syllables in sentences.* Say to the child: 'Listen and say this after me:

    (a) 'If you go out be sure to take your coat with you.'

    (b) 'When spring comes the birds begin to sing in the trees.'

One must be exactly right.

4. *Maze.* Read this slowly to the child showing him the maze. (See next page.)

(P)   'There were two rats playing together and one came to a hole in a wall. He went in there' (examiner indicates the arrow at the left of the Maze design) 'and he found his way out here, and then he came to this piece of cheese.' (Point to the cheese at the right hand of the design.) 'The other rat is hungry and wants some of the cheese too. Show me how he could find his way to the cheese. He mustn't cross any lines and if he goes up a place that he can't get out of he will be stuck because there isn't any room to turn round.'

    'Now take the pen and show me where he went to get the cheese. Draw it for me like this.' (The tester moves the pen from the nose of the rat just around the first turn in the maze, then hands the pen to the child and tells him to proceed. (The pen must be dry.)

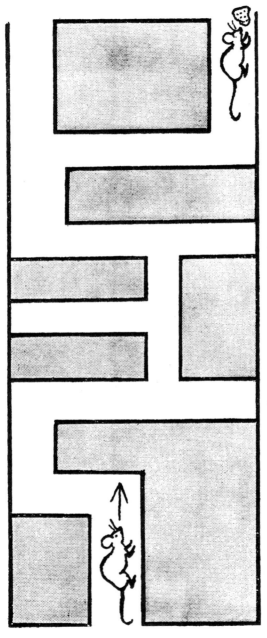

Two trials allowed in this test. If a mistake is made the tester may show the child that the way is blocked before giving the second trial. The maze must be traced without one wrong turning.

There is no need to do the maze for age 4 ; o before doing this. Here, and with later mazes, see that the child does not get his hand over the maze so that he cannot see the whole of it.

*5. *Repeating four numbers*. Say: 'Listen and say these numbers after me.' The numbers should be read at the rate of one per second. Hold up your hand and say: 'Don't start until I put my hand down.'

8, 3, 6, 1. If wrong give more trials with other numbers.
2, 4, 7, 9.   6, 1, 5, 3.
The test is passed if *one* is right out of three trials.

6. *Triple order.* Say: 'Do you see this key?' Go and put it
on that table. Then shut the door. After that bring me
(**P**) the book on that chair near the door. Do you understand?
First put the key on the table, then shut the door, then
bring me the book.'
All these orders must be carried out in this sequence
without further hints.

7. *Story word completion.* As the original form of this test
was likely to be harder for children in the centre of a big
city than for those in the suburbs or in rural areas, two
alternatives are given below, 'A' for city children and
'B' for suburban or rural schools.
Say: 'I'm going to tell you a story. Sometimes I shall
ask you to help me to make the story up. Listen.' Now
read slowly, but in a lively manner, the following, pausing
at the blanks on a questioning note, and adding if necessary, 'What do you think?'
Make a note of each reply so that you can consider
them carefully for scoring at the end of the test.
The words in the footnotes are suggested as good
answers.

A, for City Schools
'It was a very fine day; the sky was . . . . (1). The sun
was very . . . . (2). John and Mary went to walk in the
streets and bought some . . . . (3). They loved to see the
nice things in the shop . . . . (4). All at once the sky
became quite dark; it was covered with great big . . . . (5).
The little boy and girl hurried back to the . . . . (6). But
before they got there, there was a great . . . . (7). They
were very frightened by the noise of the . . . . (8). They
ran to a shop and asked if they could shelter there as it
was pouring with rain, and they had no . . . . (9) and their
clothes were quite . . . . (10).'

Suggested answers

(1) blue, bright, clear; (2) hot, bright; (3) sweets, toys; (4) windows; (5) clouds; (6) bus, house, shelter; (7) storm, downpour, burst of thunder, rain, noise; (8) thunder; (9) coats, umbrella, macintoshes; (10) wet, thin, soaked.

B, for Suburban and Rural Schools

'It was a very fine day; the sky was . . . . (1). The sun was very . . . . (2). John and Mary went to walk in the fields and picked some . . . . (3). They loved to hear the sweet songs of the little . . . . (4). All at once the sky became quite dark; it was covered with great big . . . . (5). The little boy and girl hurried back to the . . . . (6). But before they got there, there was a great . . . . (7). They were frightened by the noise of the . . . . (8). They ran to a farm and asked if they could shelter there as it was pouring with rain, and they had no . . . . (9) and their clothes were quite . . . . (10).'

Suggested answers

(1) blue, bright, clear; (2) hot, bright; (3) flowers; (4) birds; (5) clouds; (6) bus, house, shelter; (7) storm, rain, downpour, noise, burst of thunder; (8) thunder; (9) coats, umbrella, macintoshes; (10) wet, thin, soaked.

Five blanks filled in sensibly score the full mark. Four blanks score ½.

The test can be stopped when the five are scored.

Any word which makes good sense counts. Thus for B (3) anything which grows in a field (or likely to be bought in a shop by children). For (5) and (8) 'aeroplanes' may be accepted under present war conditions.

8. *Definitions by use.* Ask: 'What is a spoon? What is a chair, a table, a horse, a bed?'

Definitions by use (e.g. a spoon 'to eat with', a chair 'to sit on', a horse 'it draws a cart') is characteristic of five-and six-year-olds. Definition by class or description comes later, but, of course, should be accepted here, e.g. a horse, 'an animal', or 'it has four legs'. Much depends upon the word chosen to define.[1] If the child seems to be amused as though he thinks it a silly question, say, 'Suppose you met a little boy who did not know what a spoon was and he asked you "What is a spoon?" what would you say?' Three at least to be defined by use or description. *Apparatus needed:* Pencil and paper, pen.

TESTS FOR AGE 6 ; 0

*1. *Describing Pictures.* Provide two pictures (additional to the one given for age 3 ; 6, No. 1) which you are sure are also understandable to a child of five or six in his particular environment—e.g. a street scene with shops, motor cars, houses, etc.; a house scene with children playing and cat sleeping; a country scene with a man and dogs driving sheep along (for children in a rural area); a shop scene with some one buying; a playground scene with little children playing different games. The pictures will be more interesting if coloured. Show the picture provided and say: 'Look at this picture and tell me all about it.' At 6 ; 0 there should be more than the naming of single objects. There should be phrases describing actions, indicating the bringing of two things into relation, or an interpretation of something, e.g. 'A woman going into a shop'; 'There's a horse pulling a cart'; 'There's a big dog sleeping by the fire'; 'A boy is throwing a ball'. To score, this must be done for at least two of the pictures, or three such phrases must be used about *one* picture.

*2. *Repeating numbers.* Say: 'Listen and say these numbers after me: 5, 2, 9, 4, 7.' If wrong give a new set, 3, 5, 8, 1, 6. If the child still fails, give a third trial 7, 9, 2, 4, 3. If still wrong give a fourth trial 6, 3, 5, 8, 7. The numbers should be read at the rate of two a second. Hold up your hand and say: 'Don't start till I put my hand down.' One right scores.

---

[1] See the author's *Psychology of Early Childhood*, 3rd edition, p. 457.

3. *Funny Animals Test 'A'*

These funny animals are called Wagwums.

These funny animals are called Foozles.

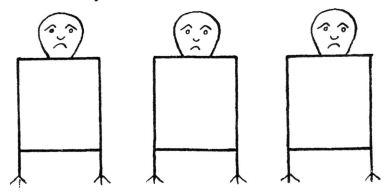

Procedure. Say (pointing) 'These funny animals are called "Wagwums", and these (pointing) funny animals are called "Foozles". Have a good look at them and see if you can tell me the difference between these and these.' After a pause ask, 'Do you know what "difference" means?' If the child says, 'No', say, 'Well, tell me what these Foozles have that these others haven't got'. When one difference is given say, 'Anything else? Can you find another difference?'

Scoring. Any correct difference counts one point. It is enough to say, for example, 'Foozles have no ears'; the child need not add 'Wagwums have ears', but if he does it scores an extra point the first time only this kind of addition is made.

The differences are as to (1) ears, (2) legs, (3) arms or paws, (4) noses, (5) shape of body, (6) mouths (e.g. open and shut), (7) teeth, (8) Wagwums look happy. Allow also (9) Foozles have only half a head, and (10) Wagwums have more claws.

Four points score 1. One point scores ½.

4. *Funny Animals Test 'B'*

(i) After doing Test 3 the child is told, 'All Wagwums (pointing to them on Test 3), have only one leg and no noses. Now look at this (below). Is this a Wagwum?'

Allow the child to refer back to the originals.

If the answer is 'No' ask 'Why?'

(ii) Say: 'Look at the Foozles again' (pointing). 'No Foozles have arms and none have ears. Now look at this (below).'

Is this a Foozle?

If the answer is 'No' ask 'Why?'

Scoring

B   (i) If the answer is 'Yes' score 0.

If the answer is 'No' ask 'Why?'

One mark for each thing pointed out as wrong ('has two legs', 'has a nose'). Maximum 2.

B   (ii) Scoring as for B (i). ('Has arms' and 'has ears'). Maximum 2.

Total maximum for Test 4 is 4 marks.

The test is passed if two marks are gained, whether both on *one* of the parts (Bi or Bii) or one on *each* part.

1 mark scores ½.

Do not tell the correct answer at any point, just say 'Yes' encouragingly.

5. *Differences.* Say: 'You know what milk is, don't you? And you know what water is? They are not the same, are they? In what way are they not the same? Tell me the difference between (*a*) milk and water, (*b*) a man and a dog, (*c*) wood and glass.'

The test is passed if one out of the three is answered. Any real difference scores. If a child only says, for example, 'A man talks', it is taken to imply that a dog does not and this is a difference; i.e. the test is passed

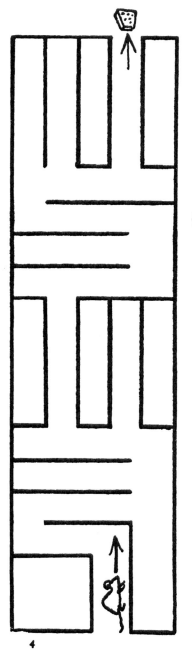

4

whenever one peculiarity of one of the pairs is mentioned. Start alternatively with (*a*), (*b*) and (*c*) with successive children to lessen the likelihood of the next testees being told about the question by one who was successful with the first pair.

6. *Maze.* No demonstration is to be given for this age, but **(P)** the child should first be given the Maze Test for 5 ; 0 if not done before. Two trials allowed. Repeat that no wrong turning must be made. If the maze is done only on a second trial score ½.

*7. *Repeating 16 syllables.* As in an earlier test (for 2 ; 6 No. 7) but now 16 syllables are required.

(*a*) We are going for a walk; will you give me a nice walking stick?

(*b*) I wish I was out in a field with a jolly dog to play with.

(*c*) In the street there are lots of motor cars and some people walking.

Two to be repeated exactly.

Opposite analogies. Say, 8 emphasizing the word underlined:

(a) A brother is a *boy*; a sister is a . . . . (if necessary, after a pause, add: 'What is a sister?')

(b) In the daytime it is *light*; at night it is . . . .

(c) Father is a *man*; mother is a . . . .

(d) A snail goes *slowly*; a rabbit goes . . . .

(e) The sun shines during the *day*; the moon shines at . . . .

Four to be given to score. Allow for such varieties as these: (a) little (or big) girl, (b) dark time, (c) lady, girl, (d) faster, quick, speed, etc., (e) night-time.

*9. *Triangles and Rectangle*. Get two cards about the size of a large visiting card, or about 2 inches by 3 inches; blacken one with pencil on one side and then divide it **(P)** diagonally into two triangles. Place the cards on the table thus:

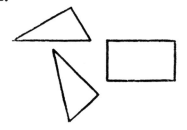

On the left of the undivided card put the two triangles, as shown, with blackened sides down. The longest sides be roughly at right angles to each other. Then say: 'One of the cards has been cut in two. Put these pieces' (pointing to the triangles) 'together to make a whole one like this' (pointing to the uncut card). N.B. The triangles must be placed as above.

If card is turned over, turn it back and say: 'No; keep the black side underneath.' When child seems satisfied, start again whether right or wrong.

Passed if *two* trials right out of three.

10. *Sentence completion*. (i) Say: 'To-day I heard a man say to his little boy, when the boy was going out: "It's

raining hard, Johnny, so . . . ." (then I could not hear the rest). What do you guess was the rest of what he said?'

Repeat this three times in all if necessary.

(ii) 'A little girl ran in from the garden and said to her mother: "My hands are dirty because . . . ." What was the rest of what she said?'

Repeat this three times if necessary.

(iii) 'A boy, having his tea, said to his mother: "Mother, this tea is too hot so . . . ." What do you think was the rest of what he said?'

Repeat three times if necessary.

Score 1 if all of the three sentences are completed in a sensible way, indicating that 'so' or 'because' was understood, e.g. for (i) 'So don't go out'; (iii) 'so let it cool', but for (ii) 'because there is dirt all over them' would not be allowed.

Ignore grammatical errors. Two right score ½

Apparatus needed: Two pictures, two small cards, pen.

TESTS FOR AGE 7 ; 0

1. *Adding money.* Arrange three pennies and three half-pennies in a circle, pennies and halfpennies alternating. Say: 'Count this money and tell me how much there is altogether.'

No repetition of instructions and no errors are allowed. Answers may be either 'fourpence halfpenny' or 'nine halfpennies'.

Time limit—15 seconds.

2. *Maze.* No demonstration is to be given for this age; but the child should first be given the Maze Tests for 5 ; 0 (P) and for 6 ; 0 if not done before. Turn the book sideways and say: 'Here is a garden. You go in here' (pointing to the S) 'and you have to come out here' (pointing to the second arrow). 'You must not make *one* wrong turning. If you do it counts wrong; and you must not turn back even a little way or lift your pen.' (A dry pen is to be used.)

A second trial may be given but the mark is then only ½.

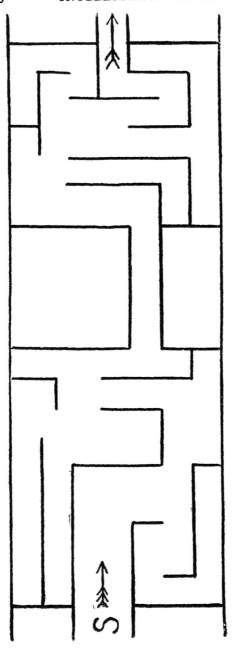

3. *Similarities.* Ask:

(*a*) In what way are *wood* and *coal* alike?

(*b*) In what way are an *apple* and an *orange* alike?

(*c*) In what way are a *ship* and a *motor car* alike?

(*d*) In what way are *iron* and *silver* alike?

Repeat the question if necessary or add: 'How are they the same?' If a difference is given for (*a*) say: 'No, I want you to tell me how they are alike. In what way are wood and coal the same?' Passed if two are answered correctly out of the four. One correct scores ½. Any real likeness is accepted. (Terman and Merrill even allow 'Both got the letter "O"').

4. Missing Features. Start with the faces — not the figure. Say: 'Look at this face. What is left

(P)   out?' After the first attempt pass to the second and third
and fourth figures. For the figure, point to it and say:
'What is left out in this?'
The test is passed if *three* are answered correctly. Do
not penalize for saying 'an ear is missing' in the second
face or in the figure.

5. *Opposite analogies.* Say:
(*a*) A brother is a boy; a sister is a . . . .
(*b*) A table is made of wood; a window is made of . . . .
(*c*) A bird flies; a fish . . . .
(*d*) The point of a stick is thick and blunt; the point of a
knife is . . . .
(*e*) A mouse is small; a horse is . . . .
All five answers to be correct for a mark. Allow also
(*a*) little girl, (*b*) glass and wood, (*c*) floats, (*d*) keen,
sharper, pointed, (*e*) big, large (but not tall).

*6. *Reasoning.* Say to the child: 'Here is a little puzzle.
There is an easy question at the end. Read it through
aloud to me, and then read it again, and try to think of
the answer, and tell me. Don't hurry; take your time.'
Read it with the child if he needs help, or if necessary
read it to him several times if he wishes.
'It looks like rain, but I shall stay indoors to-day.
Shall I want an umbrella to-day?'
When the child gives his answer, whether right or
wrong, ask: 'How do you know? Explain why.' The
explanation must be enough to ensure that the answer, if
right, was not a mere guess. If the answer was wrong,
trying to give the reason may lead to the child seeing his
error. You may say: 'Try again', and again ask the
reason.

Scoring:
1st *trial* Answer right and good reason *Score* 1
  „   „   „   „ bad   „   „   ¼
  „   „   wrong   „   0

2nd trial Answer right and good reason *Score* ½ (additional
to ¼ if
scored on
1st trial)

„   „   „   „ bad   „   „ 0

„   „   wrong   „ 0

3rd trial   „   right „ good   „   „ ¼ (additional
to ¼ if
scored on
1st trial)

„   „   „   „ bad   „   „ 0

„   „   wrong   „ 0

Maximum score = 1

7. Repeating three numbers backwards. Tell the child: 'I am
going to say some numbers and I want you to say them
backwards. If I say 3—2—6 *you* would say 6—2—3. Be
sure you say the numbers backwards. Listen now.'

(*a*) 3—6—4. (*b*) 9—1—5. (*c*) 4—7—2.

Read the numbers out steadily at about one per second
and without emphasizing one of them.

The test is passed if *one* series out of the three is
correctly repeated.

8. *Reasoning.* Instructions and scoring as for Test 6 above.

Tom said to his sisters: 'Some of my flowers are buttercups.' His sisters knew that all buttercups are yellow.
So Mary said: 'All your flowers must be yellow.' Grace
said: 'Some of your flowers must be yellow', and Rose
said: 'None of your flowers are yellow.' Which girl was
right?

Apparatus needed: Three pennies and three half-
pennies, pen.

TESTS FOR AGE 8 ; 0

1. Reading and Reproduction. Say: 'Will you read this for
me?' Point to the passage below and give the child time
to read it; say, 'I will help you with the difficult words.'

Allow two seconds pause after reading, then cover the passage and say: 'Tell me what you have been reading about.' Give the child as much help as he needs in reading.

Three Houses on Fire
London,
September 5th.

A big fire last night burnt down three houses in the middle of the city. Seventeen families now have no homes. The loss is more than 150,000 pounds. A young barber, who saved a baby in the cradle, was badly burnt about the hands.

Ignore misreadings. Count the number of items reproduced, the items being those separated out in the lines below.

Three | Houses | on Fire.| London, | September 5th. | A big | (fire) last night | burnt down *or* destroyed (three houses) | in the middle of the city. | Seventeen families | now have no homes. | (The loss is more than) 150,000 pounds. | A young barber | who saved a baby | in its cradle, | was badly | burnt | about the hands. |

Note down the exact number of items correctly reported, as the score may be needed for tests at 9 ; 0 and 10 ; 0. The test is passed at 8 ; 0 if *two* items are correctly reported. (At 9 ; 0 *six* items should be recalled, at 10 ; 0 *eight* items.)

*2. *Counting Backwards.* Say: 'You can count, can't you—1, 2, 3 and so on? Now do you think you can count backwards? Begin at 20 and go on till you reach 'one.' Like this—20, 19, 18 . . . .'
(Do not help any further.) One self-corrected error is allowed.

3. *Maze.* Say: 'Start here and find your way out.' Indicate
(P) the starting-point but *not* the exit. If the child asks: 'Is this the way out?' reply 'There is only one way out and you must find it yourself.'

The Maze Tests for 5 years (No. 4) and for 7 years (No. 2) should be given for practice if not already done. Scores ½ if done only on second trial.

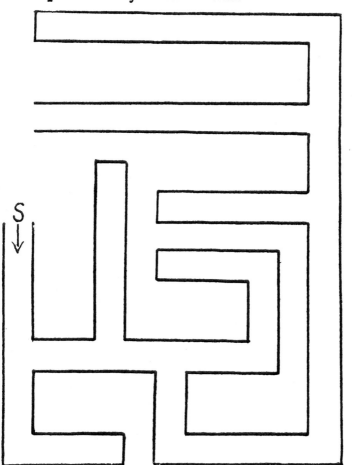

4. *Reasoning.* Say: 'Try to do this puzzle.' Then read the passage below slowly to the child several times. Let him follow the words on the page if he can read. Procedure and scoring as for 7 ; 0, Test 6:

'It is Sunday and on Sunday afternoon Ada usually

takes the baby out, or goes by herself to the pictures, or walks over to see her aunt, or else goes by tram to the cemetery. To-day she has no money with her, and the baby is asleep upstairs. Where do you think she has probably gone?'

5. *Opposites.* First make sure that the child understands what 'opposite' means. Say: 'Tell me the opposite of these words: "Good".' If child does not reply, say: '"Bad" is the opposite of "Good",' and go on: 'Tell me the opposite of "Asleep".' Again tell him if he does not answer correctly, and so with 'Great' and 'Strong' and 'Careless' till he gives at least two correctly. If he does not by now know enough to give a true opposite he fails the test.

Now say: 'Tell me the opposite of these words' and read out each of the list below, waiting for a reply to each. Allow about seven or eight seconds for each of the first ten and then about five seconds, if necessary, for each of the rest—completing in three minutes.

Ten should be done correctly for this test to score; eight correct score $\frac{1}{2}$.

Old, poor, big, early, long, easy, inside, pretty, boy, wet, kind, winter, woman, slow, white, upwards, loud, crooked, cheap, busy, sunrise, brother, borrow, clean, common, warm, tight, mountain, father, true, shut, female, few, heavy, multiply, absent, moving, question, now, polite, east, enemy, nobody, glad, top, possible, come, front, day, tame.

6. *Relations.* Say: 'I'm going to ask you an easy question. Don't guess too quickly; let me read it several times first.'
   (i) A daddy and mummy had three children, Mary, Kate and Rosy. How many sisters had Mary? (Read over three times slowly before allowing the child to answer.)
   (ii) Another daddy and mummy had three children, John, Sally and Elsie. How many sisters had Sally? (Read three times.)

(iii) How many sisters had John? Remember there were three children, John, Sally and Elsie. (Read three times.)

1 mark if all three are correct; ½ mark for two correct.

7. *Reasoning.* Instructions as for 7 ; 0, No. 6:

(a) John is bigger than Ted. Ted is bigger than Bob. Who is the biggest? (Read over three times slowly before allowing the child to answer.)

(b) Jane is fatter than Mary, and Kate is fatter than Jane. Who is the fattest? (Read three times.)

(c) Tom runs faster than Jim. Jack runs slower than Jim. Who is the slowest, Jim, Jack, or Tom? (Read three times.)

All to be answered correctly. If one answer is wrong ask 'Why?' and if in the course of explaining the child sees and gives the right answer, count it as passed; ½ mark if two done correctly.

*8. *Answering easy questions.* Ask:

(a) 'Suppose you had to go somewhere by train. What must you do if you miss the train?'

Pass—'Wait for another', 'Take the next'. But local conditions may justify 'Take a bus' or 'Go home'.

(b) 'What ought you to do if you broke something that belonged to some one else?'

Pass anything implying restitution, apology or confession; e.g. 'Pay up', 'Own up', 'Tell mother'. Some disallow the last; but surely a little child would probably have to restore through the mother.

Fail 'Cry', 'Hide it'.

(c) 'If another boy or girl hit you by accident, without meaning to, what should you do?'

Pass 'Nothing', 'Forgive him'—anything that implies excusing or overlooking the act.

Fail 'Hit him back', 'Tell mother'.

The test is passed if two questions out of three are answered correctly.

Apparatus needed: Pen.

TESTS FOR AGE 9 ; 0

*1. *Reading and Reproduction.* As for 8 ; o, No. 1, except that now six items must be recalled to score 1 for a nine-year-old test. (The test must not be repeated. If the child scored 6 when he did it in the eight-year series, he scores for this nine-year-old test as well. If he got less than 6 he scores o.)

*2. *Definition by Class and Description.* Ask the child 'What is a horse', a 'chair', 'a mother', a 'table', a 'fork'.

Anything more than mere use (as given for the test for age 5, No. 6) scores here: for example, if a *quality* of the object is mentioned (e.g. a horse has 'got four legs') or if the object is said to belong to some class, even if the class is very general, e.g. a chair is 'a *thing* to sit on'.

Three words so defined score 1. Two words score ½.

*3. *Repeats 6 numbers* in *one* of the two series. The numbers should be read at the rate of 1 per second and without any rhythm.

$$8—2—5—3—6—9 \qquad 3—5—7—2—6—4$$

4. *Reasoning.* Procedure and scoring, as for age 7 ; o, test 6.

Peter has a half-holiday on Wednesdays and Saturdays, and a whole holiday on Sunday. I am at work all day, except on the afternoons of Monday, Wednesday, Friday and on Sunday. I want to take Peter to the tailor's to buy him a new suit. Which afternoon could we go together?

If the child says they could not go on Wednesday because it is early closing day, score a pass. If a child in a Jewish district suggests Sunday, say: 'No, all the shops are shut in this town on Sunday' and give another trial.

5. *Maze.* Before doing this test the child should be given
(P) the maze tests for 7 ; o and 8 ; o for practice.

Pointing to S in the maze below, the examiner says: 'Start here and find your way out. Mind you don't make one wrong turning.' If the child asks: 'Is this the way out?' the examiner replies: 'There is only one way out and you must find it yourself.'

Two trials can be allowed. If done only on a second trial, score ½.

6. *Analogies.* This is usually given as a group test: but for the sake of the bright seven- or even six-year-olds who can only read a little or not at all, it has been adapted as an individual test. The analogies are taken from Burt's list (*Mental and Scholastic Tests*, p. 226).

Explain this test by reading out and completing the first three examples given below for the child. Then tell him to give you the right word for the others as quickly

as he can, as you read them out. Allow him three minutes.
Nod approval as each is attempted and pass on to the
next. The child can look at the words as you read them
out to him.

Six right score 1, 4 right score ½.

(Burt gave 6 as the normal number completed by
nine-year-olds in five minutes; but that was as a *written*
group test. The main thing is to ensure that the analogy
relationships can be grasped.)

(1) Prince is to Princess as King is to ....?
(2) Pencil is to Drawing as Brush is to   ....?
(3) January is to February as First is to ....?

---

(1) Sailor is to Soldier as Navy is to ....?
(2) Moon is to Earth as Earth is to ....?
(3) This is to Here as That is to ....?
(4) Day is to Midday as Night is to ....?
(5) Little is to Big as Dwarf is to ....?
(6) Foot is to Leg as Hand is to   ....?
(7) Neighing is to Braying as Horse is to ....?
(8) Heat is to Cold as Summer is to ....?
(9) I is to Mine as You is to ....?
(10) Table is to Wood as Window is to ....?
(11) Dining-room is to Bedroom as Eating is to ......?
(12) Coffee-grounds are to Coffee-pot as Tea-leaves
        are to ....?
(13) Sheep is to Mutton as Pig is to ....?
(14) East is to West as Day is to ....?
(15) Penny is to Copper as Nail is to.................?
(16) Hour is to Minute as Minute is to ....?
(17) Bicycle is to Tricycle as Two Wheels are to .....?
(18) Straw is to Hat as Leather is to ....?
(19) White is to Snow as Black is to.................?
(20) Cloud is to Rain as Sun is to....................?
(21) Spider is to Fly as Cat is to....................?
(22) Uncle is to Aunt as Brother is to................?

(23) Liquid is to Solid as Water is to ....?
(24) Little is to Less as Much is to ....?
(25) Grandfather is to Husband as Grandmother is to..?
(26) Tuesday is to Wednesday as Wednesday is to ......?
(27) Wash is to Face as Sweep is to.................?
(28) Evening is to Morning as Supper is to ....?
(29) Tailor is to Baker as Clothes are to.............?
(30) Pale Yellow is to Deep Yellow as Pink is to........?
(31) At Home is to Abroad as England is to...........?
(32) Fire is to Hot as Ice is to......................?

Apparatus needed: Pen.

TESTS FOR AGE 10 ; 0

1. Sentence building with three words. Say: 'You see these three words—London, River, Money. Make up a sentence with these three words in it. Tell me something with these three words in it.' (The name of the nearest big town may be used instead of London.) Allow one minute only from the time you begin.

One idea or sentence indicates the eleven-year-old stage. For 10 ; 0 two sentences may be allowed, e.g. 'There is a river in London. I should like some money,' or even three if they are well co-ordinated in meaning, e.g. 'London is a big town, it has a river in it; some people there have a lot of money.' Three separate sentences unconnected in meaning fail.

2. Reading and reproduction. As for 8 ; 0, No. 1, but eight items must be recalled to score for 10 ; 0 years. The test must not be repeated if it has been done before. If in a previous testing the child scored less than eight it counts as a failure for this age of 10 ; 0.

3. Drawing two designs from memory. Provide the child with pencil and piece of plain paper. Say: 'I have here two easy drawings. I shall show them to you for a very short time and then ask you to draw them both from memory. Look at *both* carefully first of all. Ready?' Now put the figures exactly in front of the child and show for exactly

10 seconds. Turn them over, hand the child the pencil and say: 'Now draw them.'

Scoring. The whole of one drawing and half the other reproduced with fair exactness, score 1; but the lines need not be straight, e.g. one square within another, with *corners* connected by straight lines is 'correct'. One square inside another, and *some* connecting lines is only half correct. The key pattern is 'half correct' if the centre hump or one *side* is omitted, or if turns at ends are reversed, or curves are put for squares at end or if whole figure is inverted. Failure if *two* of these errors are made.

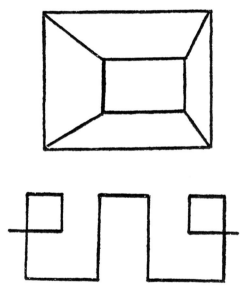

4. *Analogies.* As for 9 ; 0, No. 6, but 8 must be right to score 1. No need to repeat or continue test if 8 were scored before. If not, start now half-way down the list.

5. *Maze.* Instructions as for Maze Test for age 9 ; 0, No. 5.
(P)   The Maze Tests for 7 ; o and 9 ; o should be done first for practice. Two trials allowed as before. Score is 1 if done first time, ½ if on second trial (Turn book sideways and start at the top.)

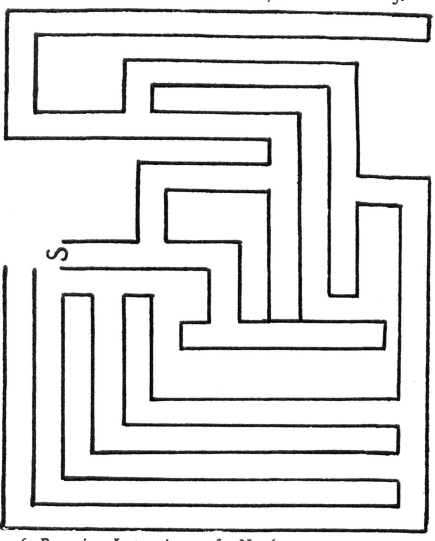

6. *Reasoning.* Instructions as for No. 6, age 7 ; 0.

If I have more than a shilling I shall either go by taxi or by train; if it rains I shall either go by train or by bus. It *is* raining and I have two shillings. How do you think I shall go?

Apparatus needed: Pen, pencil, and paper.

TESTS FOR AGE 11 ; 0

*1. *Explaining Absurdities.* Say: 'Listen carefully to what I am going to say. There is something in it that is really quite silly and impossible. See if you can tell me what is wrong.'

(i) 'One day, a man fell off his bicycle on to his head, and was killed instantly. He was taken to the hospital, and they fear he may never get better. What is there silly in that?'

(ii) 'I have three brothers—Jack, Tom, and myself. What is silly in that?' (Female examiners must substitute 'I have three sisters—Jane, Mary, and myself.')

(iii) 'Yesterday there was a railway accident, but it was not a serious one. Only forty-eight people were killed. What is silly in that?'

(iv) 'Once the body of a poor girl was found in a wood, cut into eighteen pieces. They say that she killed herself. What is silly in that?'

(v) 'A man once said: "If I should ever grow desperate and kill myself, I shall not choose a Friday to do it on; for Friday is an unlucky day, and would bring me bad luck." What is foolish in what the man said?'

THREE ABSURDITIES should be detected OUT OF FIVE.

If a child's first statement is not quite clear, say: 'Explain what you mean.' Otherwise allow no second chance.[1]

2. *Answering Problem Questions.* Say: 'Can you tell me this?'

(i) 'What should you do if you found you were late on your way to school?'

(ii) 'If some one asked you what you thought of a boy' (or, if the examinee is a girl, 'of a girl'), 'whom you did not know very well, what should you say?'

[1] Burt gives suggestions as to 'satisfactory' and 'unsatisfactory' answers to these questions, and further guidance than is given here as to the answers of the next test (Problem Questions) in *Mental and Scholastic Tests*, pp. 57, 58.

(iii) 'Suppose a boy does something that is unkind: why do we forgive him more readily if he did it in a temper than if he was not angry?'

(iv) 'Why should we judge a person by what he does and not by what he says?'

(v) 'Suppose you were going to do something very important, what should you do before you did it?'

Repeat a question ONCE, if necessary, but do not vary the wording.

THREE out of FIVE must be answered satisfactorily.

(i) *Satisfactory:* e.g. 'Hurry' or 'Run'.

(ii) *Satisfactory:* Anything that suggests the need of making an inquiry or withholding an opinion.

(iii) *Satisfactory:* Anything suggesting that anger may constitute an excuse, however badly expressed.

(iv) *Satisfactory:* Anything implying that words are more deceptive than actions, though both need not be mentioned.

(v) *Satisfactory:* Anything implying preliminary preparation as to method (reflection, practice, seeking advice or help), or preliminary consideration as to expediency or possibility.

*3. *Giving 32 words in one minute.* 'I want you to give me as many words as you possibly can in one minute. Some children can give nearly a hundred. Keep saying words like this till I stop you: box, coat, tree, cart, and so on— any words you like. Are you ready? Now start.' (If he breaks off, encourage him by saying: 'Very good, keep on.')

The statement that some can give nearly a hundred is deliberately inserted; give exactly the same four examples to every child.

Thirty-two words must be given exclusive of repetitions. If the child gives sentences, start him again, saying: 'You must give separate words.' Observe the exact time with the second hand of a watch.

* 4. *Repeating five numbers backwards.* Say: 'I am going to
say some numbers and you have to say them backwards.
If I said 6—2—3 you would say 3—2—6. Listen, and be
sure to say the numbers *backwards*.' (Read the numbers
out at one per second.)

5—2—4—9—3

If an error is made repeat the test with 2—7—4—8—3;
and, if necessary, give a third chance with 6—3—9—2—5.
One out of three scores 1.

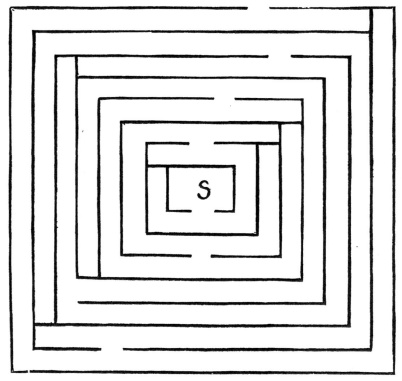

5. *Maze.* Mazes for 8, 9, and 10 years should be done for
(P)   practice if not already done. Instructions as for age
8 ; o, No. 3.
Score ½ for success on second trial.

6. *Reasoning.* 'The doctor thinks Violet has caught some illness. If she has spots it is probably chicken-pox, measles, or scarlet fever; if she has a cold or a cough, she may have whooping cough, measles, or mumps. She has been sneezing and coughing for some days, and now spots are coming on her face and arms. What do you think is the matter with Violet?'
Scoring as for age 7 ; 0, Test No. 6.
Apparatus needed: Pen.

TESTS FOR AGE 12 ; 0

1. Re-arranging mixed sentences. Say to the child, pointing to the words at A below, and covering up all below them: 'Here are some words all mixed up. Read them to me.' When they are read (with help if necessary) say, 'Now you can't understand what that means, can you? Try to put them in the right order to make sense.'

One minute only is allowed from the words 'make sense'. If the child inserts an extra word say: 'No, you must not add any words.' If he omits a word do not give a second chance.

A.   A defends
master dog good
bravely his.

Now proceed as before with

B.   My asked paper
the I teacher
correct to

If A and B are done correctly the test is passed. If neither is done correctly the test is already failed. If only one was correct proceed as before with:

C.   Started the for
morning early this
we country.

If now *two* sentences have been given correctly the test is passed.

(The latest Terman and Merrill scale puts this test at 13 ; o. I retain Burt's placing based on his London standardisation, but I would allow for A: 'A master defends his good dog bravely', of which Burt disapproved; and I would allow for C: 'For the country this morning we started early').

*2. *Reasoning.* Procedure; Say to the child 'Read this story aloud. At the end there is a question. Read the story carefully and then answer the question that it asks. If you want to, you can read the story two or three times yourself before you answer the question.' Help the child to read the story or read it to him if necessary. (Scoring as for Age 7 ; o Test No. 6.)

A man was found nearly dead with his throat cut, and on the back of his left arm there was a blood-stained mark of a left hand. The policeman says he tried to kill himself. Do you think the policeman was right?

*3. *Maze.*
(P)   Mazes for 8 and 10 years should be done for practice if not already done. Instructions as for age 8 ; o No. 3. Score ½ for success on second trial.

4. *Reasoning.* (Scoring as for age 7 ; o Test No. 6.)
Procedure: Say to the child: 'Read this puzzle aloud. At the end there is a question. Read the puzzle carefully and then answer the question that it asks. If you like you can read the story two or three times to yourself before you answer the question.' Help the child to read the story, or read it to him if necessary.

Where the climate is hot, aloes and rubber will grow.
Heather and grass will only grow where it is cold.
Heather and rubber require plenty of moisture.
Grass and aloes will grow only in fairly dry regions.
Near the river Nobbo it is very hot and very damp.

Which of the above grows there?

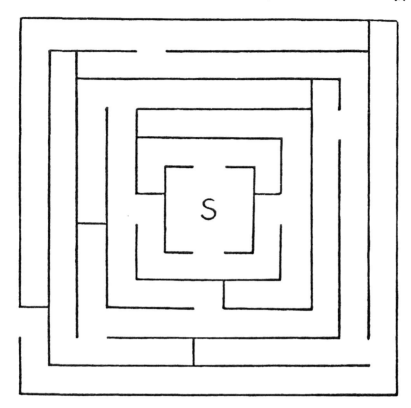

5. *Triangle and oblong test.*

Apparatus needed: an oblong of thick cardboard 6½ ins.
(P) long and 5 ins. wide. In the positions shown in the
diagram below cut out an oblong 2 ins. wide and 2⅓ ins.
long: and a triangle with a base of 4 ins. and height of
2⅓ ins. Divide into two halves the pieces cut out (the
oblong diagonally and the triangle vertically) providing
four right angled triangles as shown in the diagram. See
that the edges of the triangles are trimmed neatly so that
they will fit readily into the openings. Arrange the
material on a flat table exactly as in the diagram and say:

'These pieces have been cut out of this big card. Put them back again properly as quickly as you can. I shall time you.'

The test is passed if done correctly in 40 seconds. Score half if done in 45 seconds.

Subject seated here

6. *Opposites.* Instructions as for age 8 ; o, Test No. 5, except that now the child may be expected to read the words himself. Also allow now only five or six seconds for the first five words in the list below and then proceed more rapidly, stopping after three minutes. Thirty-eight should be done correctly to score. Thirty correct, score ½.

Less	Asleep	Forget	Complete
Great	Land	Large	Left
Love	Thin	Over	Happy
Sell	Me	Narrow	Laugh
Low	Dislike	Sober	Well
Blunt	Backwards	Tender	Stand
Yes	Wrong	Lost	Evening
Win	Near	Obey	End
There	Lowland	Soft	Little
First	Within	Nice	Slanting
Noisy	Smooth	Careless	Dark
Best	North	Town	Stale
Strong			After

Apparatus needed: Cardboard triangles etc., for No. 5, and pen for No. 3.

TESTS FOR AGE 13 ; 0

1. *Reasoning.* (Procedure as for 12 ; 0, No. 4, and scoring as for age 7 ; 0, No. 6.)

Field-mice devour the honey stored by the humble-bees; the honey which they store is the chief food of the humble-bees. Near towns there are far more cats than in the open country. Cats kill all kinds of mice. Where, then do you think there are most humble-bees—near towns or in the open country?

2. *Imitation of Movement Pattern.*

(P) Sit at a table with the child on your left, *not* opposite to him. Place four small cubes (or four cotton bobbins or four small matchboxes) in a straight row in front of the child, about two inches apart. With a fifth cube (bobbin or matchbox) tap the cubes according to the pattern given below, (one tap on each cube) about one tap per second. (The cube on the subject's left, numbered 1, is tapped first.)

Then place the fifth cube in front of the child, on a line between the third and fourth cubes, and say, 'Now do the same'.

The next pattern is now tapped and so on till the child fails in three successive patterns. Seven patterns must be done correctly to pass.

Patterns.

(a) 1 2 3 4	(e) 1 4 3 2	(k) 1 3 1 2 4
(b) 1 2 3 4 3	(f) 1 4 2 3	(l) 1 4 3 1 2 4
(c) 1 2 3 4 2	(g) 1 3 2 4 3	(m) 1 3 2 4 1 3
(d) 1 3 2 4	(h) 1 4 3 2 4	(n) 1 4 2 3 4 1

3. Reasoning. (Procedure as for Age 12 ; o, No. 4, and scoring as for 7 ; o, No. 6.)

I started from the church and walked 100 yards; I turned to the right and walked 50 yards; I turned to the right again and walked 100 yards. How far am I from the church?

4. *Analogies.* Instructions as for Test 6, Age 9 ; o, except that now the child may be expected to read the test himself. To score at this age 21 analogies should be given in four minutes; 15 score $\frac{1}{2}$.

If the pupil has already done the test, as given for 10 ; o and then scored 21 or more, there is no need to repeat the test. If he scored less, begin now with the item No. 13 (p. 48) and continue if necessary, with the items given below. If the test is now being done for the first time begin with item No. 1 on p. 48.

Pale Yellow is to Deep Yellow as Pink is to...........?
At Home is to Abroad as England is to.............?
Fire is to Hot as Ice is to ....?
Cork is to Water as Balloon is to....................?
Robin is to Swallow as Winter is to..................?
Man is to Woman as Boy is to.......................?
Steamer is to Pier as Train is to....................?
Sky is to Blue as Grass is to........................?
Once is to One as Twice is to.......................?
Cat is to Fur as Bird is to...........................?
Library is to Books as Greenhouse is to.............?

Gulf is to Sea as Cape is to........................?
Houses are to Bricks as Cathedrals are to...........?
Three is to One as Yard is to.....................?
Oyster is to Shell as Banana is to...................?
Good is to Bad as Long is to......................?
Eat is to Bread as Drink is to.....................?
James is to Jimmie as William is to.................?
Seeing is to Eye as Hearing is to...................?
Fruit is to Orange as Vegetable is to...............?
Lily is to Flower as Oak is to.....................?
Trunk is to Elephant as Hand is to.................?
Sit is to Chair as Sleep is to.......................?
Half-Sovereign is to Gold as Bullet is to.............?
Cradle is to Baby as Stable is to...................?
England is to London as France is to...............?
Small is to Large as Mouse is to...................?
Eat is to Fat as Starve is to........................?

5. *Absurdities.*

Say to the child. 'Some of these sayings are sensible and some are absurd and silly. Read them and tell me which are sensible and which are absurd.'

(*a*) A soldier writing home to his mother said: 'I am writing this letter with a sword in one hand and a pistol in the other.'

(*b*) 'Ada' and 'Eve' are two names that are spelt the same way backwards and forwards.

(*c*) A man said to his shoemaker: 'You stupid man; I told you to make one of the shoes larger than the other, and instead of that you have made one of them smaller than the other.'

(*d*) A boy said he would be glad when he grew up as then he would be more able to do as he liked.

(*e*) I am not conceited, for I don't think I am half as clever as I really am.

(*f*) The three men laughed; then stopped suddenly as the eyes of each met the others across the table.

(*g*) Every rule, even this one, has an exception.

Two of the absurdities must be detected and reasons given clearly enough to show it was not guess work. The reply to the items (*b*) and (*d*) are ignored.

*6. *Reversing Hands of a clock.*

Say to the child: 'Think of a clock. Suppose it is 23 minutes past six, can you picture in your mind where the large hand would be and where the small hand would be?' Children of 13 nearly always say 'Yes'. Even if they sound doubtful, proceed. 'Well, suppose the two hands of the clock now change places; the large hand is where the small hand was and the small hand is where the large hand was. What time would it be now? Remember, it was 23 minutes past six.

The test is done correctly if the answer is 4.30 or anything up to 4.35. The child is not allowed to look at a clock or watch or to draw a clock. There is a time limit of two minutes.

Repeat the test with the hands at 8.13: the answer to this is correct if it is given as forty minutes past two or anything up to 45 minutes past two. If one and one only of these examples is done correctly, give a third test with the hands at 2.51 saying nine minutes to three. The answer to this would be correct if it is between ten past ten and a quarter past ten, inclusive.

Two of the tests must be done to score.

Apparatus needed: five cubes (or bobbins) for No. 2.

TESTS FOR AGE 14 ; 0

1. *Code Test.* Say, 'Here is a message from a spy, which has been written in a secret code. This, (showing it to the child), is what the writer wanted to say:'

A B L E   T O   C O M E

And here it is in code:

b c m f   u p   d p n f

'In the secret message' (pointing to it) 'each letter stands for a particular letter in the alphabet—b for A, c for B, and so on.' (The examiner points to each letter as he reads it.)

'You want to send another message in the same code. What you want to say is: "Fly, all is discovered". See if you can write it out in the secret code.'

(The test is passed if there are no more than two mistakes in the child's attempt. Score ½ if three mistakes are made.)

*2. *Maze.*

(P)

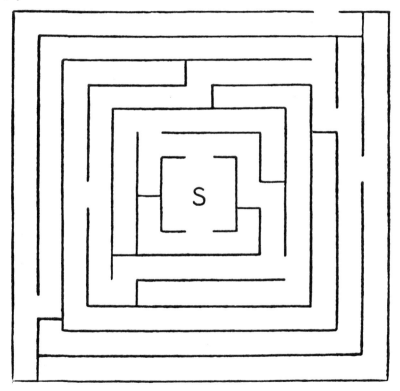

Mazes for 8, 10, and 12 years should be done for practice if not already done. Instructions as for age 8 ; 0, No. 3. Score ½ for success on second trial.

3. *Reasoning.* (Scoring as for age 7 ; o, Test No. 6, and Procedure as for Age 12 ; o, Test 4.)

A pound of meat should roast for half an hour; two pounds of meat should roast for three-quarters of an hour; three pounds of meat should roast for one hour; eight pounds of meat should roast for two hours and a quarter; nine pounds of meat should roast for two hours and a half. From this can you discover a simple rule by which you can tell from the weight of a joint how long it should roast?

4. *Drawing a reversed triangle.*

(P) Prepare an oblong card, about 10 by 5 cm. (4 by 6 inches). Cut across the diagonal, as shown below, but without the letters marked on it. The card is first laid on the table before the child with the cut edges touching. Do not let the child see the figures below.

Procedure. Say, 'Look carefully at the lower piece of this card. Suppose I turn it over and lay this edge' (pointing to line AC *without moving the card*) 'along this edge' (AB of the upper triangle); 'and suppose that this corner' (C) 'is placed just at this point' (B); 'what would it all look like. Now I am going to take the piece away' (remove the lower triangle from view). 'Imagine it placed as I told you; and draw its shape in the proper position. Begin by drawing the shape of the top of the triangle.'

Evaluations. The essential points are (i) ACB must be preserved as a right angle; (ii) A'C must be shorter than AB.

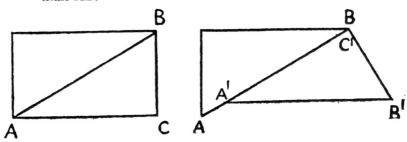

5. *Absurdity Test.*

Say, 'This story is full of ridiculous and impossible statements—words or phrases which contradict each other or the rest of the passage. Some persons found twenty or thirty absurdities. Read it through first and then read it again and tell me the words or phrases which you think are absurd.' No time limit is imposed.

A Sunday in France[1]

Ten years ago on a pleasant summer's afternoon in the middle of January, 1916, the twelve o'clock express from Scotland was rushing past the busy terminus of the Great Western Railway at twelve miles an hour.

A clean-shaven young Englishman, of about fifty years of age, stepped lightly from one of the first-class carriages and hurried slowly down the platform with both hands in his pockets, carrying a heavy bag, and gaily curling the tips of his moustache. His strange voice suggested that he was a native of Germany, born and bred no doubt in France; and by his dusty shoes I gathered he had walked over from America that very morning.

There was not a cloud in the sky; and, as the rain was still falling heavily, he took off his mackintosh and strolled out into the crowded streets of the city. The ripening fields of corn through which he passed were turning golden as the sun set in the south. The square semi-circle of the new moon shone brightly in the heavens overhead. The evening shadows grew shorter and shorter in the twilight. And a few minutes later, with a burst of splendour, the day dawned.

He was standing on London Bridge watching the grey waters of the Severn rush northwards out to sea, and listening to the bleating of the sheep on the Welsh mountains. A few feet above his head an aeroplane was standing still in the sky; and beyond in the cloud a bright

---

[1] Taken with some modifications from Burt's *Mental and Scholastic Tests*, 2nd edition 1947, p. 249.

red seagull, with its four wings outspread, could be seen flying invisibly above the Dutch mountains. The clock, on the dome of St. Paul's struck the hour. 'One, two, three,' he counted, and then ten more strokes. 'It must be just half-past eleven,' he said, 'no wonder I am thirsty. I must call at the greengrocer's for a glass of salt beef.' Twenty absurdities must be pointed out to score; no reasons need be given.

6. *Practical problem.*
'A man goes round with a cart selling oil from a large barrel. Most of his customers ask for either 8 pints or 5 pints, and he has one can which holds exactly 8 pints and another can which holds exactly 5 pints. But one customer wanted just 3 pints. Can you tell me how the man measured out exactly 3 pints by using his two cans? *Apparatus needed:* Card for No. 4, and pen for No. 2.

TESTS FOR AGE 15 ; o

*1. *Reasoning.* (Procedure and scoring as for age 7 ; o, Test No. 6.)
John said: 'I heard my clock strike yesterday ten minutes before the first gun fired. I did not count the strokes, but I am sure it struck more than once, and I think it struck an odd number.' John was out all the morning, and his clock stopped at five to five the same afternoon. When do you think the first gun was fired?

2. *Maze.* (See opposite page.)
(P)   Mazes for 10, 12, and 14 years should be done for practice if not already done.

*3. *Repeating six numbers backwards.*
Instructions as for Test 4 for 11 ; o. *One* out of the three sets to be repeated correctly.
5—7—2—8—1—4, ...   3—5—9—4—6—2, ...
6—1—4—7—3—8.

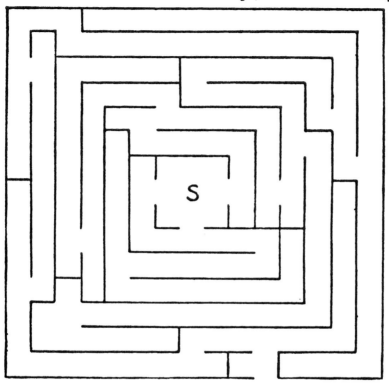

4. *Reasoning*. (Procedure and scoring as for age 7 ; 0, Test No. 6.)

Mary has just taken a penny ticket. The trains from this station all stop at Euston, but after that some go to Chalk Farm and Golders Green; others go to Kentish Town and Highgate. They stop nowhere else. The fare to Euston, Chalk Farm or Kentish Town is a penny; to Highgate or Golders Green, twopence. Mary did not get in the Golders Green train or get out at Euston. To what station do you think she is travelling?

5. *Reapeating 26 syllables*.

Say: 'Listen and say this after me: say *exactly* what I say.'

6

(*a*) The other morning I saw in the street near home a tiny yellow dog which had no chain or collar on.

After noting the score on (*a*) proceed similarly with (*b*) and, if necessary, with (*c*).

(*b*) We should never be cruel to birds because they are such weak defenceless things, and are so sweet and pretty.

(*c*) In our school we have lots of books but I should like more with pictures in them, and I should like to take them home.

Two must be repeated exactly, with the words in the same order.

6. *Drawing from imagination the cuts in a folded paper.*

(P)

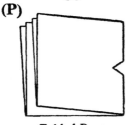

Folded Paper
(*a*) as shown

Prepare two sheets of paper about 6 inches square. One sheet should be folded in four like a letter ready for an envelope, and reopened. In the middle of the edge which presents but a single fold a small triangular notch, about 1 cm. deep, has already been drawn. (See Figure (*a*).)

Say to the child, 'Here is a sheet of paper that I am going to fold into four.' (The examiner refolds the paper while the child watches.) 'Suppose now I cut out a notch, just here. When the paper is unfolded again, what would it look like? Will you show me on this other piece of paper how and where it would be cut?'

The examiner places the folded paper in front of the child with the corner showing the folds towards the child, and the pencil-mark uppermost and visible. The child must not touch the paper shown to him, nor fold the other sheet. (Beware of saying 'draw the *holes*,' as this of itself indicates that more than one hole is required; and great care must be taken that the child does not catch a glimpse of Figure (*b*) given on the next page.

To pass the test, two diamond-shaped holes should be drawn in a line with each other, one near the centre of each half of the paper. (See Figure (*b*).) It does not matter whether the drawings of the holes lie in a horizontal or in a vertical straight line.

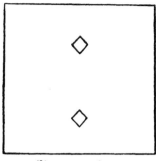

(*b*) as reproduced

Note if the child has been helped by special previous experience, e.g., a course on paper folding.

Apparatus needed: pen for No. 2, pencil and two square pieces of paper for No. 6.

APPENDIX

I. SELECTION OF, AND INSTRUCTIONS FOR TESTS

I take the view that, with very young children—say 2 ; 0 to 6 ; 0 or 7 ; 0—such factors as interest, the mood of the moment, the personality of the tester, etc., have such a great influence, that it is more important to have a large number and variety of tests than to have a small number with more precise instructions as to marking.

In the Terman and Merrill tests the instructions for marking are very elaborate: lists of answers which should be accepted or rejected sometimes occupy two or more printed pages for one test. This, of course, has great advantages when an exact comparison has to be made between two groups of children tested by different persons, or when it is desired to get the exact I.Q. of a child, based on the results of the particular set of tests.

The method, however, has certain disadvantages: first it cannot hope to be complete; some border-line answers may still remain doubtful, and indeed some classed as wrong by Terman and Merrill seem to me to be as good as some accepted by them. More especially the very detailed instructions considerably lengthen the time consumed in testing and marking, at least until the tester is thoroughly experienced with the tests.

It seems to me preferable to save time by having fewer instructions and spend it in giving a greater number and variety of tests: especially as, in the majority of cases, it is really fairly obvious whether the test is passed or failed. Hence the provision here of 10 tests for each half-year period from 1 ; 6 to 3 ; 0 and of 8 from 3 ; 6 to 8 ; 0, instead of the usual half-dozen.

II. TESTS OF GENERAL AND SPECIAL ABILITIES

In spite of (or perhaps I should say 'because of') our ignorance as to how far special abilities have developed at these very early ages (especially 2 ; o to 4 ; o or 5 ; o), it is advisable to include as great a variety of tests as possible. Some of the group factors indeed (e.g. language and number) are so important that tests which depend not only on general abilities but also on the most important group or special abilities, may, for the practical purposes of school progress and the wider work of later life, be more useful than a test of pure 'g'—even if we could find one.[1]

For the sake of interest, and to lessen the influence of home teaching in language, a good proportion of our tests for the earliest years are performance tests or at least involve very little language. The Porteus Maze tests are given right up to the age of 15 ; o. I share Burt's views as to the value of these tests as a supplement to other types.[2]

III. THE PLACING AND STANDARDIZING OF THE TESTS FOR AGES 4 ; o TO 8 ; o

As the reader will have concluded from the Introduction I have followed Binet's principle in the placing and standardizing of the tests, as Burt did in his revision of the Binet Scale.

Nearly all the tests I have given had already been widely standardized. A substantial proportion of the tests for the ages 3 ; o up to 9 ; o and 10 ; o are included in Burt's revision of the Binet Tests (as given in *Mental and Scholastic Tests*) or in his later list which includes some of the Stanford Revision Tests (as given in Burt's *Subnormal Mind*, p. 350). A few other tests are placed by the widely standardized Terman and Merrill Tests. The Porteus Maze Tests have already been well standardized by Porteus and later by

[1]As to special abilities involved in tests of the Binet type, see 'The Factorial Analysis of the Terman-Binet Tests', by C. Burt and Enid John, *Brit. Jour. of Educ. Psych*, Vol. XII, 1942.

[2] *Mental and Scholastic Tests*, 2nd edition p. 254. In *The Backward Child*, Burt states that he thinks the Porteus Maze to be the best single Performance Test where time is limited. As to Performance Tests in general it is notable that Godfrey Thomson found one set to correlate as highly 0.7 with Stanford-Binet Tests see *An Analysis of Performance Test Scores of a Representative Group of Scottish Children* (1940).

Burt. Those given here are, with slight modifications, the latest revised forms and standardizations by Porteus.[1]

It should be noted that in both the Binet and the Terman-Merrill Tests, a test, say test (a) for 6 ; o, may be easier than one (b) for 5 ; o.[2] But this does not matter if the particular group of tests for a certain age is suitable as a whole. Also, nearly all children of 5 ; o will do the 6-year tests too (and the six-year-olds will do the 5-year tests), so for these children it does not matter where tests (a) and (b) are placed.

The placing of all these tests has been further checked by the results of the direct application of the present set. For this purpose I have the results on 414 children for the ages 4 ; o to 8 ; o distributed as follows:

Age 4 ; o—55   Age 7 ; o—118
Age 5 ; o—99   Age 8 ; o—43
Age 6 ; o—99

As each year-group of tests would be applied also to those one year above that year as well as to most of those one year below, this makes about 250 to 300 children for each year-group of the tests for 5, 6, and 7 years.

These children were nearly all in unselected Infant and Junior Schools, almost all in or near Birmingham, except for a group of about 25 who were in a rural area. Of the Birmingham Schools, one was in a poor district and provided about 175 of the children. (Thirteen decidedly subnormal children in this school were not included in the results.) Three schools were in suburban districts and provided about 65 children. The remainder of about 150

[1] See his book, *The Maze Test and Mental Differences* (Vineland, New Jersey, 1933). I thought the Porteus tests at 3 ; o, and 4 ; o, were too much tests of hand steadiness, so the figures for these two ages were made wider than Porteus made them, but slightly more complicated, involving an entrance and exit, in order to make the tests partly instruction tests. I have also, with Burt, allowed ½ for success on 2nd trial.

[2] See Burt's Table III, p. 144 of *Mental and Scholastic Tests*; also Q. McNemar, *The Revision of the Stanford-Binet Scale* (Boston, U.S.A., 1943), p. 84.

were in fairly average schools, about a score being in Nursery Schools.

In this final checking of the placing of the tests I have followed Burt's criterion that a test should be passed by 50 per cent of the children in the age group *below* that to which the test is assigned.[1] A further check is the percentage of the children of a given age passing the tests assigned to their age. This, Burt has shown, should decrease as we pass from younger to older age groups, being about 78 per cent at 5 ; o, about 72 per cent at 8 ; o, and about 62 per cent at 11 ; o.[2]

How closely the results of my tests approximate to Burt's criterion is shown by the following figures:

TABLE

Tests	Percentage Passing (at age *below* that to which tests are assigned)			Percentage passing (at age to which tests are assigned)	
For age 4				80 per cent	
For age 5	53 per cent pass at 4 ; o			76	,,
For age 6	53	,,	,,	5 ; o	72	,,
For age 7	[3]57	,,	,,	6 ; o	80	,,
For age 8	[4]68	,,	,,	7 ; o	75	,,
For age 9	51	,,	,,	8 ; o		

[1] Op. cit., 2nd edition, p. 152.

[1] See the Table, op. cit., p. 144. I have averaged the percentages for each year.

[3] This 7-year score is not based on the full number of tests, as I abandoned the use of two tests at a late stage in the testing, namely 'Adding number of fingers on the hands' and 'Drawing a diamond shape'. The former was abandoned because of the danger of the influence of special training, the latter because of the difficulty of standardizing the marking. Instead of these I introduced two other tests, (a) 'Repeating three numbers backwards', placed at 7 ; o in both Burt's Revision and the new Terman and Merrill Scale, and (b) a Burt's Reasoning Test (in my present set No. 8 for age 7 ; o). As this proved a rather difficult test compared with the others for age 7 ; o it helped to reduce the previous easiness of the tests indicated by the percentages given in the Table above. If all the tests are included in the calculation (with due weighting for the reduced numbers of children tested with the new tests) the average percentage of passes is just below 50 per cent.

[4] The performances of seven-year-olds on eight-year-old tests and on their own 7-year tests are high because a large proportion of the seven-year-olds were over 7 ; 6 (86 out of 118). I should like to repeat, however, that the main justification for my placing of the tests is that the great

IV. NEW TESTS

In this series of tests there are only four new tests of my own—the two 'Funny Animals' Tests (Nos. 3 and 4 for age 6 ; o), the 'Sentence Completion' Test (age 6 ; o, No. 10), and the 'Relations' Test (age 8 ; o, No. 6). Several other tests, however, involve some modifications of the originals, namely, one of Burt's Reasoning Tests and the adaptations of his Opposites and Analogies written tests for use as individual oral tests.

My object in devising the 'Funny Animals' Tests (see pages 32 to 34) was to make a test which would arouse interest and even amusement (as it almost invariably does), which would involve little use of language, be uninfluenced by school instruction, and test the fundamental process of perception of differences (Test No. 3) and the grasping and applying of a definition or generalization (Test No. 4).

These tests were first tried on a group of about 100 children, ages about 5 ; o to about 7 ; 6, mostly in Infant Schools, with a few in Private Schools. On the basis of these preliminary experiments the tests were assigned to age 6 ; o, and further results (in the three Birmingham Schools mentioned above) have fully justified this. Indeed, few of the tests show so marked a rise in the scores for the ages assigned over the year before it. The total number of children tested in these further trials was about 270 and the scores were as follows:

Funny Animals Test

	Age 5 ; o	Age 6 ; o	A ; o
Number of children	97	99	77
Percentage passing:			
Test 3	58	74	99
Test 4	38	69	92

majority of them have already been widely standardized by previous investigators. I might add that Mr. B. B. Wakelam, who applied the tests to over 250 children between the ages of 4 ; o and 8 ; o, in his own school, found that the standard deviation was about 11·5. (See his article on 'The Application of a New Intelligence Test in an Infant School, and the Prediction of Backwardness', *Brit. Jour. of Educ. Psychology* Vol XIV, 1944.)

It may be noted that the *average* percentage (for the two tests) passing at 5 ; o is 48 per cent—very close to Burt's requirement of 50 per cent. The rapid rise in passes from 5 ; o to 6 ; o and again from 6 ; o to 7 ; o is also a good feature in a test like this in which no special training at school can account for a sudden rise.

Sentence Completion Test for age 6 ; o. This simple test was devised to ascertain at what age the child could grasp the relationship implied in the conjunctions 'so' and 'because'. I was stimulated to experiment because I felt sceptical about Piaget's statements as to the young child's inability to grasp such relations. The test was tried first on the same hundred children used for the preliminary trial of the Funny Animals Test, and on this basis assigned to age 6 ; o. In the further applications in the three Birmingham schools, the following results were gained which justify the allocation:

	Age 5 ; o	Age 6 ; o	Age 7 ; o
Number of children	97	99	77
Percentage passing	51	80	90

Relations test for age 8 ; o. This was at first also planned to check Piaget's assertions as to the age at which reciprocal relations are grasped. It was first applied to some 95 children chiefly in Infant and Junior Schools and assigned to age 8 ; o. In further applications in the three Birmingham Schools the following results were obtained:

	Age 7 ; o	Age 8 ; o
Number of children	115	43
Percentage passing	62	79

(The percentage passing at 7 ; o is rather high, but considerably more than half these seven-year-olds were over 7 ; 6.)

Burt's Reasoning Tests

To fit some of these into the Binet scheme which I have followed needed some slight adjustment; but I was very anxious to use some of the Reasoning Tests in view of their high correlation with general intelligence.

For allocating the Binet Tests, Burt holds that the best criterion for placing a test on the Binet scale is that 50 per cent of the children of the age *below* the particular year should pass that year's test. Thus if half the eight-year-old children pass a given test that test is just suitable for nine-year-olds.[1] I have applied this criterion of Burt's to his own Reasoning Tests. Thus as half the children of 7 ; 0 years are expected by Burt to do the test over the 7 ; 0 line in Burt's list, these tests are given in my list for the eight-year-olds.

I have made an alteration in one of Burt's Tests, namely that placed here at age 8 ; 0, No. 7. I thought it very difficult for a child to give reasons for answers to this test, without being merely tautologous; on the other hand, to mark for a right answer only to the one question given by Burt would leave a big element of chance. Hence I give three questions instead of Burt's one, and require all to be right for a full mark, but no reasons are asked for.[2]

The placing of these Reasoning Tests in my selection scale is based chiefly, as I have indicated, on Burt's own extensive standardization; but it is confirmed, first by a comparison with scores for the other tests for each particular age, and

---

[1] For a full account of Burt's arrangement of his Reasoning Tests see his *Mental and Scholastic Tests*, p. 249. I am able to add that Professor Burt approves of my placings.

[2] Burt bases his short list (in *Mental and Scholastic Tests*) on a longer series of Reasoning Tests (see *Journal of Experimental Pedagogy*, Vol. V, 1919, and Ballard, *Mental Tests*). For my test No. 8 at 7 ; 0, I have used a test listed by Burt at 7 ; 0 in his long list which he perhaps would have placed after the 7-year line, and so on my plan should have been an 8 ; 0 test: but I was anxious to have a second Reasoning Test for age 7 ; 0, and as the rest of the group of tests for 7 ; 0 seemed slightly easy, it was an advantage to add a rather difficult test. As this Reasoning Test (No. 8 for 7 ; 0) was a late addition to my tests I have too few results to be worth quoting.

second as judged by Burt's own criterion given above. These are the figures:

		At 6 ; 0 %	7 ; 0 %	8 ; 0 %
Test here assigned to 7 ; 0—No. 6 passed by		42		
„ „ 8 ; 0—No. 4 „			57	
„ „ 8 ; 0—No. 7 „			55	
„ „ 9 ; 0—No. 4 „				49
Number of children		95	118	43

As Burt points out (p. 250) with these tests 'there is at any one age a far greater range of individual variation than with the Binet-Simon Tests'. They sort out very decidedly the high-grade defective and the brilliant child may score far beyond his age.

New Adaptation of Two Group Tests

Opposites Test for 8 and 12 years. This is Burt's group test[1] adapted as an oral individual test. The meaning of 'opposites' is first explained, as Burt suggests, by preliminary examples.[2] Burt found the average score for age 8 was 10·2 words written in five minutes. To adapt it as an individual test, usable for six- and seven-year-olds and for backward readers, I required 10 opposites to be given orally in three minutes, ½ being scored if 8 were given. The results were as follows:

	Age 7 ; 0	Age 8 ; 0
Number of children tested	115	43
Percentage passing	73	79

The percentage passing at 7 ; 0 is high but over two-thirds of these were over 7 ; 6 and this percentage of 73 is actually less than the average score of these seven-year-olds on the three widely standardized tests I have included for age 8 ; 0 from Burt's revision, viz. Reading and Reproduction, Counting Backwards, and Answering Easy Questions, which was 76 per cent.

[1] *Mental and Scholastic Tests*, 2nd edition, p. 235
[2] Op. cit., p. 233.

Analogies Test for 9, 10 and 13 years. This group test has also been adapted as an individual test; as prescribed it can be used as an oral test, which is an advantage as it will be required for the brighter seven- or even six-year-olds who would probably be seriously handicapped if they had to read the test. I have used Burt's list of Analogies. He gives 6 as the average number of analogies written down correctly by nine-year-olds in five minutes;[1] for my individual test the time is reduced to three minutes as no writing has to be done. My own standardization of this test is very incomplete but it fits in closely with the placing of my other nine-year-old tests; thus the average scores on all my nine-year-old tests are as follows: for seven-year-olds 44 per cent, for eight-year-olds 52 per cent, while the results for my adaptation of the Analogies Test for age 9 ; o were as follows:

	Age 7 ; o	Age 8 ; o
Number of children tested	95	43
Percentage passing	42	50

V. THE VALIDITY AND PROGNOSTIC VALUE OF TESTS AT THE AGES OF 1 ; 6, 2 ; 0, AND 3 ; 0

In the Introduction (pp. 4, 11), I have mentioned the risk that the performances of young children (especially those below the ages of 4 ; o and 5 ; o) may be influenced by emotional moods, by the attitude of the child to the tester, and by the intermittent nature of mental development. I also referred the reader to a summary of results of investigations as to the prognostic value of tests at 1 ; o and 2 ; o, given in my *Psychology of Early Childhood*. Since the publication of that book an important investigation of the prognostic value of tests at 2 ; o, 3 ; o, and 4 ; o has been reported by F. L. Goodenough and K. Maurer in *The Mental Growth of Children from Two to Fourteen Years* (University of Minnesota Press, 1942). They found the correlation of performance on the Minnesota Tests at 2 ; o with Stanford-Binet Tests at 6½, 7½, and 8½ varied between 0·4 and 0·45.

[1] Op. cit., p. 250.

The correlation of I.Q. at 3 ; o based on the Minnesota Tests with I.Q. at 8 ; 6 based on the Binet Tests, was 0·64 and at 9 ; 6 it was 0·65—higher than the correlation between the Minnesota Tests and the Merrill-Palmer Tests at the *same* ages of 3 ; o and 4 ; o and higher even than the correlation between the Minnesota Tests under 3 ; o and those over 4 ; o—which was 0·53.

This seems to emphasize the unreliability of only *one* testing at the early age of 3 or 4, rather than the changes in I.Q. over a period of five or six years—from 3 to 8 or 9.

When the results of the Minnesota Tests at 3 ; o were compared with those gained with the Terman-Merrill Tests (1937) at 7 ; o to 12 ; o, the average correlation was about 0·5 for 168 children (p. 80). With larger numbers for the testing at 4 ; o and at 7 ; o, the correlation rose to 0·68 and between age 4 ; o and ages 8 ; o to 13 ; o the correlation varied from 0·43 to 0·73.[1]

These correlations, of course, allow for large individual variations (p. 80), but on the whole Goodenough and Maurer claim that the tendency is for the child's I.Q. to remain fairly constant.

Further correlations of testings at early ages with I.Q.'s and performance at the adolescent stage have still to be made. Here are research problems of great interest. But the main practical problem for the teacher of the Infant and Junior School is: 'What is this child capable of in the next two or three years at school?'

VI. SELECTION AND STANDARDIZATION OF TESTS FOR
AGES 1 ; 6, 2 ; o, 2 ; 6, AND 3 ; o

For tests at 1 ; 6 I have relied chiefly on Gesell's placing, with a few confirmations by the Merrill-Palmer findings. For tests at 2 ; o I have again largely followed Gesell's placing with due consideration of the Merrill-Palmer findings in several of the tests and of Terman and Merrill's

---

[1] In a more recent investigation it was found that the I.Q.'s obtained (even on only one testing) at the ages of 2 and 3, correlated at 12 or 13 to the extent of 0·66. See K. P. Bradway, "Predictive value of Stanford-Binet Pre-school Tests,' *Amer. Jour. of Educ. Pysch.*, Vol. XXXVI, 1945.

placings in four tests. Where there is a difference in placings by two authorities I have usually made a slight adjustment in requirements for passing, which results in a compromise. At 2 ; 6 the placings of Gesell, Merrill-Palmer, and Terman-Merrill have been followed again with a few compromises. At 3 ; o one comes to more suitable tests in the Binet scales, including the revisions by Burt and Terman; but here and at 3 ; 6 I have still made some use of Gesell's tests and findings.   Apart from the Porteus Maze Test for 3 ; o (fully standardized by Porteus himself), the placings of practically all the tests at these ages have the support of two and sometimes of three wide investigations. Here again, where the placings by other investigators have differed I have sometimes made a slight adjustment in the test, especially in the scoring. Here and in some of the later tests I have tried to lessen the element of luck, e.g. by giving some choice but requiring a bigger score, and occasionally I have lessened the error due to personal judgment of the tester, by allowing half a mark for some partial or doubtful answer. Although nearly all these tests have been already widely standardized by previous investigators, yet as I have been able to check the present tests *as a group* on so few children of 2 ; o and 3 ; o, I cannot feel the same confidence in the placing for the tests given from 1 ; 6 to 3 ; 6 as for the ages 4 ; o and over, and I shall be specially grateful for any results which competent testers obtain if they would kindly send them to me.

VII.   TESTS FOR AGE 12 ; O TO 15 ; O

Of these tests added in the third edition of this book a number are Binet tests justified by the wide standardizations of Burt and Terman. I have also again made free use of Burt's Reasoning, Analogies, and Absurdity Tests. In addition to the mazes and Binet's 'Drawing of reversed triangle', I have included two other interesting performance tests: the 'Triangle and oblong test',[1] and

[1] As adapted by Frances Gaw (from Pintner and Paterson's '*A Scale of Performance Tests*', D. Appleton & Co., 1917) in her Report on *Performance Tests of Intelligence*. (Industrial Fatigue Research Board, 1925.) Norms of performance are given on p. 33.

the 'Imitation of Movement Pattern (The Knox Cube Imitation Test).[1]

I have selected a group of items from Ballard's Absurdity Tests appropriate to the age of 13, according to his standardization.[2]

In these tests for the higher ages I have avoided those on defining abstract terms because of the difficulty in assessing answers.

In the present (fifth) edition I have added for age 14, a practical reasoning test in a form kindly supplied by Sir Cyril Burt as specially standardized by him for that age.

For age 15 there is now added another non-verbal test, making two non-verbal tests for age 15, as there are for age 14. This test is from Burt's revision of the Binet Tests (*Mental and Scholastic Tests*, 2nd edition, p. 64). I have made a few verbal alterations. For the Code Test (Age 14, No. 1 in the previous editions) I have substituted an improved form of Code Test, also provided by Professor Burt and standardized by him for Age 14.

As it is widely agreed that general ability increases only slightly after 15 or 16 even in the abler persons, and probably ceases to mature before that age in the duller ones, these tests may be regarded as covering mental development almost up to full maturity.[3]

[1] See also Gaw's *Report*, p. 15. Norms on p. 33.

[2] See P. B. Ballard 'The Limit of the Growth of Intelligence' *Brit. Journ. of Psych.* Vol. XII. I selected one test from each of Ballard's five grades, and took as a basis his average score for the better-type elementary school, which was approximately two-fifths of the maximum of the 34 tests. This average was somewhat better than the average in one elementary school in a poorer district, but lower than that in a central school, the average for which would be equivalent to about 2½ out of 5.

[3] It may be noted that the latest Terman and Merrill scale passed from 14-year-old tests to those for 'Average Adults.'

BOOKS ON INTELLIGENCE TESTS RECOMMENDED FOR FURTHER STUDY

R. Knight. *Intelligence and Intelligence Testing.* (London, Methuen, 1933.)

C. Burt. *Mental and Scholastic Tests.* (London, 1933.)
The Backward Child, Chapter III. (London, 1937.)

C. W. Valentine. *Psychology and its bearing on Education*, Chapters XXIII and XXIV. (Methuen, 1950.)

R. B. Cattell. *A Guide to Mental Testing.* (London, 1936.)

J. Drever and M. Collins. *Performance Tests of Intelligence.* (London, 1936.)

A. Gesell. *The Mental Growth of the Pre-school Child.* (New York, 1925.)
The First Five Years of Life. (London, Methuen, 1942.)

H. R. Hamley (Editor). *The Testing of Intelligence.* (London.)

R. Pintner and D. G. Paterson. *A Scale of Performance Tests..* (Appleton.)

L. W. Terman and M. A. Merrill. *Measuring Intelligence.* (London, 1937.)

R. Stutsman. *Mental Measurement of Pre-school Children*, (New York, 1931.)

INDEX

LIST OF APPARATUS

In envelope, published separately (see p. v).

For Age 2 ; o Test 5.	Formboard and three insets. (Also for use at ages 2 ; 6 and 3 ; o.)
For Age 3 ; o Test 7.	Garden path.
For Age 3 ; 6 Test 1.	Three pictures.
Test 2.	Sketch of dog, cut in half and sketch of horse, cut in half.
Test 4.	Four Squares each, of white, black and red paper.
Test 8.	Card with geometric figures printed on it, and paper packet with ten figures on separate cards.
For Age 4 ; o Test 1.	Card with parallel lines.
Test 6.	Maze on card.
For Age 5 ; o Test 4.	Maze on card.
For Age 6 ; o Test 3.	Funny Animals on card.
Test 4.	Funny Animals on card.
Test 6.	Maze on card.
Test 9.	Cards of rectangle and two triangles, black on one side.
For Age 7 ; o Test 2.	Maze on card.
For Age 8 ; o Test 3.	Maze on card.
For Age 9 ; o Test 5.	Maze on card.
For Age 10 ; o Test 5.	Maze on card.
For Age 11 ; o Test 5.	Maze on card.
For Age 12 ; o Test 3.	Maze on card.
Test 5.	Cardboard oblong and four card triangles to fit gaps.
For Age 14 ; o Test 2.	Maze on card.
Test 4.	Card oblong cut into two triangles.
For Age 15 ; o Test 2.	Maze on card.